For Debbie
With lots
Mom and Dad

Sermons of
Arthur C. McGill

Sermons of
Arthur C. McGill

Theological Fascinations
Volume One

ARTHUR C. MCGILL

Edited by
David Cain

Foreword by
William F. May

Cascade Books
A division of *Wipf & Stock Publishers*
199 West 8th Avenue, Suite 3 • Eugene OR 97401

SERMONS OF ARTHUR C. MCGILL
Theological Fascinations, volume 1

Cascade Books
A Division of Wipf & Stock Publishers
199 W. 8th Ave., Suite 3
Eugene, OR 97401

ISBN 10 : 1-59752-917-6
ISBN 13: 978-1-59752-917-4

Cataloging-in-Publication data:

McGill, Arthur Chute.
Sermons of Arthur C. McGill / Arthur C. McGill ; edited by David Cain.

xiv + 160 p.; 23 cm. — (Theological Fascinations; v. 1)

ISBN 10: 1-59752-917-6
ISBN 13: 978-1-59752-917-4

1. Sermons, American—20th century. I. Cain, David William, 1941–. II. Title. III. Series.

BV4253 .M28 2007

Manufactured in the U.S.A.

With appreciation to Gordon D. Kaufman and the *Harvard Gazette* for permission to publish the "Memorial Minute."

For Arthur McGill and Lucy McGill in gratitude.

Contents

Acknowledgment

I welcome this opportunity to honor Art and his work. His sermons were refreshing, inspiring interpretations of Scripture. He had a unique ability to find meaning which made the Scriptures come alive and become more relevant for daily living. His thoughts were different from the usual presentations.

It was when I was involved in his early writings, typing them, that I began to appreciate his thoughts and how complex and different they were. He had always shared with me the reactions of those who heard his sermons and lectures. How I enjoyed that! I was so happy for him.

Thank you, Art, for giving me enlightenment and joy. I treasure those experiences.

—Lucy McGill, 2006

Foreword

Where would a preacher go if he wanted to expose to view the powerlessness of words? If he were bold—with a dash of David, Amos, or Daniel in his genes—he would probably go to Harvard University, the citadel of words, where the most verbal of men and women pour out words in the classroom, dress parade them in their books, and, in exchange for tuition money, produce graduates who will build careers and try to master their lives through the mastery of words.

In the following collection of sermons, Arthur C. McGill chose a Harvard Convocation as the time and place to offer a disquisition on the powerlessness of words to tame and manage the powers that beset us. He recognized that an age which is "unbelievably verbal" has, in fact, lost confidence in the power of words. An uneasy resourcelessness underlies our talkativeness. We plunge ahead into the next sentence, because we recognize the vacuity of the last sentence. The world we live in reeks of turbulent powers that overmaster us and do not submit to the routines of shared discourse–the highway accident, a report on lethal lab values, love turned sour, or the devastations of war, so confounding that "Those conducting the war have shown no capacity to explain its purpose. Those who oppose the war are so filled with revulsion and horror that they, too, seem incapable of formulating a policy that makes practical sense" (Sermon 10, p. 90).

This distrust of speech drives preachers as much as other *Wordmeisters*. Pulpiteers press on ahead with yet one more paragraph, one more illustration, one more theatrical pause, because, in their heart of hearts, they know that they have not achieved a decisive breakthrough, a word that truly empowers, heals, and transforms in the midst of the unruly powers that beset them and their congregations.

McGill's Harvard address, like so many sermons in this collection, approaches Scripture attentively in the hope that the Word of God will break through the terrible isolation of our impotent wordiness and conjoin God's power with human speech. He asks us to attend to the text with him and to open ourselves up to the alterations in our sensibility which the Word may entail. Scripture doesn't offer a rhetorical illustration of a universe already familiar to us but a realm that revises our understanding of both speech and power. Such speech is self-communicating; such power is self-expending love. Therewith speech and power conjoin.

Scripture brings before us speech that is not isolating, devoid of power, because we discover in Scripture the speaker who in full measure extends himself, opens himself, explains himself to others, puts himself at their disposal. In such speech, the word becomes deed; the self-communicating word is self-giving. The speaker did not come to chatter, but to die. Jesus Christ enables human speech itself to become the medium of God's power, the power of self-expending love.

Thus the Harvard Convocation closes with a call "to recover speech with power . . . to take it out of the classroom and reroot it in the realm of painful deeds" (Sermon 10, p. 95).

Professor David Cain, a student of Arthur McGill's at Princeton University, has painstakingly assembled this convocation and collection of sermons out of penciled notes, written in the urgency of each occasion. One does not have the impression that preaching was an extra-curricular add-on for McGill, an exercise to which preaching has been reduced by many theologians in academic life. Rather preaching marks out a proving ground where one wrestles with the Word, with some hope for a hearing that blesses.

It is not accident, I think, that David Cain has taken on both Søren Kierkegaard and Arthur McGill in his own scholarly work. The stunning reversals of ordinary wisdom in McGill's sermons remind one of the earlier prophet's "Thoughts on the Present Age" and his "Attack upon Christendom." Both men open up a very rough terrain. However, a huge difference distinguishes the two men. For Kierkegaard, the Incarnation, the Word made flesh, does not, in one sense, breach the gulf between the divine and the human. God in human form is still an incognito. God does not reduce to the prior categories of human knowledge. That God has crossed the gulf between the divine and the human requires a leap of faith into the unknown; and each person leaps across that gulf on his or her own. The earlier prophet mocks, goads, and prods each to make that leap, one by one.

McGill proceeds differently in all of these sermons, even on such polyglot an occasion as a University Convocation. He attends to the Word in the hope that God would cross the gulf in both the speaking and the hearing. A faithful hearing is not simply human knowledge, but it is a knowledge. In Jesus Christ, God's power, God's self-expending love, conjoins with human speech. "Is it not precisely the meaning of the grace of God in Jesus Christ that the fullness of power—God's power—is shown to be compatible with human speech, with human community as a community of shared consciousness? . . . God's power, when it enters into our existence, does not shatter what is human . . ." (Sermon 10, p. 93). So understood, a hearing does not summon each into a void. A hearing is a "convocation"; that is, a hearing together, which "implicates our concrete actual life in the life of others" (Sermon 10, p. 94).

David Cain's introduction to this collection honors that element of hearing together. He does not, like many editors, treat McGill's writings as a finished piece of work, placed in his hands, which he then proceeds in McGill's absence to introduce to others. The introduction itself unfolds as a two-way conversation not only with possible readers but with McGill himself. No teacher could hope for more.

—William F. May

Introduction
"Some Real Surprises"[1]

Sermons of Arthur C. McGill

*For there is no distress like that of believing in something
which you secretly know may be false. (Sermon 6, pp. 58-59)*

Arthur Chute McGill, Christian theologian, teacher, and preacher, reigned
in the classroom. He was a paced master of dialectical surprise. He possessed
a passionate honesty. He knew the *risk* of faith. McGill was intellectually
tough: he would not believe something he secretly knew to be false. With no
proof that the Christian faith is true, he was clear that there is no proof that
it is false. But wait: "*may* be false"? To believe in something which you *know*
is false: yes, grave distress. But to believe in something which you "know may
be false" but which also may be true: surely such honesty belongs to the risk
of Christian confession. Is the "may be false" in the quotation above probability—not possibility? Even so, probability does not rescue one from risk when
the probability is of—improbability. Why, then, risk improbability? McGill's
sermons and surprises offer response to this question.

Meet McGill:

- But if you cease to hope, to live on the edge of hope, like a child alert
  for the coming of Christmas, then you die. (Sermon 15, p. 129)

- Because the mind is the greatest narcotic, it is extremely difficult for
  any of us to know our suffering, especially the deep suffering that
  belongs to our daily life. (Sermon 2, p. 30)

---

[1] Sermon 17, p. 141. McGill is referring to the so-called parable of the good Samaritan:
"Tonight we will concentrate on one parable of Jesus, the parable of the Good Samaritan. It is
not only an interesting story, but it has some real surprises." I apply his phrase to his sermons.
References to McGill's sermons are hereafter in text: (Sermon #, p. #).

- Jesus died—he died all the way . . . (Sermon 3, p. 34)

- Any person who is not willing to be emptied, to let go of his own piety and his own faith and his own loving and his own virtue, he is full of extortion and rapacity, full of spiritual pride and greed. (Sermon 3, p. 37)

- Love is the name for the frame of mind, for the attitude which does not mind being poor. (Sermon 3, p. 38)

- You measure the meaning of letting go by the power of Christ and not by the power of death. (Sermon 14, p. 121)

- The proper speech is the deed. (Sermon 10, p. 95)

- The price of ecstasy is poverty. (Sermon 6, p. 61)

- It is always strange, this message of Jesus, to everyone everywhere . . . (Sermon 12, pp. 106–7)

- If you love, you will be used up. (Sermon 9, p. 84)

- We do not first love our neighbor, first our neighbor loves us. (Sermon 17, p. 146)

In what might be read as a commentary on the above quotations, McGill proposes:

> "Faith" is not the possession of a settled world-view ["viewpoint Christianity"], which people can interpose between themselves and the shock of experience, and by which therefore they can keep the world at an arm's length away from them, can solve all their problems, and can arrange themselves with the "right" attitudes for every situation. On the contrary, "faith" has the effect of *opening* a man to the world, to his neighbors, and to himself. It deprives him of all self-conscious postures. It propels him into a living engagement with concrete experience.[2]

The Stuck Imagination

"American life is in the midst of some deep and obscure torment" (Sermon 6, p. 53). So preaches Arthur McGill about 1974—and about today. McGill's words leap into our present—any present, surely—but so patently and painfully into our own. Here is McGill's declaration in context:

> Nothing makes clearer why this is a moment of deep disquiet and anxiety. For all the conflicts and frustrations which beset our life in

[2] Arthur C. McGill, *The Celebration of Flesh: Poetry in Christian Life* (New York: Association, 1964) 14; see 187–90, "Against Spiritual Pride."

the United States today make it difficult to face the future with assured enthusiasm. American life is in the midst of some deep and obscure torment. (Sermon 6, p. 53)

McGill speaks of "American life today" from the 1960s and 1970s, of the Vietnam War and "mimeographed reports" (Sermon 10, p. 87). "Friends, as the daily news reports to us the pains and agonies of the whole world, let us keep each other awake. Let us hope not in the future, but in the God who will [bless?] every [possible?] with the fullness of his glory and his love" (Sermon 15, p. 129). McGill suggests that "the problem of policy" in the context of Vietnam is not bound to that context:

> It has to do with the general conviction in American life today that when real power is unleashed, we are beyond the realm of speech. For that reason, I would expect that if we were to become embroiled in Czechoslovakia or in the Middle East in a war of savage destruction [*if we were to become embroiled . . .*], we would find ourselves burdened by the same anguish. (Sermon 10, p. 90)

The "anguish" referred to is the anguish in the gap between words about and devastation in Vietnam.

William F. Lynch imagines, "In eternity there will be . . . less stuckness in the imagination,"[3] indicating his own unstuck imagination. In the company of Aeschylus' *Oresteia*, Lynch dramatizes imagination as "trapped," "stuck," stuck with "no way out," "puzzled," "caught."[4] Lynch and the "stuck" imagination: if our imaginations were "stuck" when Lynch wrote (1970), they are downright reified today. Have our imaginations ever been more trapped?[5] McGill would resonate with the idea of our stuck imaginations. His sermons may be read as attempts to unstick our imaginations, to unglue them, to open them up, to turn them loose, to set them and us—with and because of them—free.

McGill looks around in his today and in his past and ours to the poor and oppressed, the poor of Brazil, pygmies of Africa, the ancient Chinese, to the Indian, to Vietnam, Czechoslovakia, the Middle East, India, to the South, Selma, to Harlem, Chicago, Watts. What the topical references exemplify is still exemplified; what they deplore is still deplorable.

---

[3] William F. Lynch, SJ, *Christ and Prometheus: A New Image of the Secular* (Notre Dame: University of Notre Dame Press, 1970) 136.

[4] Ibid., 85, 87.

[5] A temptation is to look about from "today" and to sound a myopic or at least immediate alarm. But when does "temptation" become obligation?

"Truth Is Meant to Save You First,
and the Comfort Comes Afterwards"

In Georges Bernanos' magnificent novel, *The Diary of a Country Priest*, an old, seasoned, earthy priest, M. le Curé de Torcy, strives to help initiate a young, naive country priest of the village of Ambricourt:

> Teaching is no joke, sonny! I'm not talking of those who get out of it with a lot of eyewash: you'll knock up against plenty of *them* in the course of your life, and get to know 'em. Comforting truths, they call it! Truth is meant to save you first, and the comfort comes afterwards. . . . The Word of God is a red-hot iron. And you who preach it 'ud go picking it up with a pair of tongs, for fear of burning yourself, you daren't get hold of it with both hands. . . . when the Lord has drawn from me some word for the good of souls, I know, because of the pain of it.[6]

These words become powerfully ironic when, later in the novel, the country priest thrusts his arm into a fire. He is "no tongs." So is Arthur McGill, whose dialectic is heavy on what he risks as the truth and light on the "comfort"—as if, in light of the truth, the comfort can take care of itself: "Truth is meant to save you first, and the comfort comes afterwards." The truth can be painful, which is why we are so tempted to do an end run around the truth and to go straight for the comfort. A student once gave me a poster—it was on my office door for years—which showed a rag doll with bright yellow yarn hair going through the ringers of an old-style washing machine. Her tongue was hanging out. The poster read: "The truth will make you free, but first it will hurt like hell." "The Word of God is a red-hot iron."

Much of the fire for McGill comes from what Karl Barth called, in the title of an early address (1916), "The Strange New World within the Bible."[7] Strangeness and newness can be fearful and frightening—and exciting, exhilarating. Barth wonders:

> Whence is kindled all the indignation, all the pity, all the joy, all the hope and the unbounded confidence which even today we see flaring up like fire from every page of the prophets and the psalms? . . . We might do better not to come too near this burning bush.[8]

McGill risks it. Barth continues:

---

[6] Georges Bernanos, *The Diary of a Country Priest*, trans. Pamela Morris (New York: Carroll & Graf, 1983) 54.

[7] Karl Barth, *The Word of God and the Word of Man*, trans. Douglas Horton (New York: Harper & Brothers, 1957) 28–50.

[8] Ibid., 30, 32.

> . . . within the Bible there is a strange, new world, the world of God.
> . . . The paramount question is whether we have understanding for
> this different, new world, or good will enough to meditate and enter
> upon it inwardly. . . . Time and again serious Christian people who
> seek "comfort" ["comfort" again] and "inspiration" in the midst of
> personal difficulties will quietly close their Bibles . . . the Bible . . .
> offers us not at all what we first seek in it.[9]

Barth's essay exudes excitement and exhilaration: "It is not the right
human thoughts about God which form the content of the Bible, but the
right divine thought about men."[10] McGill, far from running tired or dry,
exudes theological fascinations. No "apologies," no arguments for biblical
authority or truth. The real truth, the "true truth," is authoritative and needs
no defense. Defense is insult. Defense is betrayal. McGill risks and dares
boldly—hence the energy and vitality of his thought.

Never is Arthur McGill far away from death. Never does it take him
long to get to death; and, as we recognize however reluctantly with our apprehension of the acceleration of time with age, it does not take us long
either. Death, death, death. McGill, in his "realistic," unrelenting way is aim-
ing at affirmation. "Truth is meant to save you first, and the comfort comes
afterwards." There is death, and there is death.[11] There are different concepts
of death—more than two, certainly; but let us focus on two. There are destructive death and creative death. Destructive death is demonic, the death
of victimization, obliteration, extermination. This is what sin and the satanic
have somehow done to death. Then there is death as donative, self-giving,
death as letting loose and letting go, a creative death which is essentially a part
of the dialectical dance of receiving and giving which is life—as in the life of
the living, Trinitarian God in whose image we are created. McGill does not
like the first kind of death (any more than you and I), but he faces it in his
McGillian realism in order to press through to death two:

> So long as there is death, the power of God is not primary, is not
> Lord. Where there is death, there is not God's kingdom. Therefore the
> Christian lives under death, or rather against death. Not against death
> by a more secure having, but against the whole logic and metaphys-
> ics of having and of the death which gives the metaphysics its proof.
> (Sermon 14, p. 120)

---

[9] Ibid., 33, 37, 39.

[10] Ibid., 43.

[11] See David Cain, "Arthur McGill: A Memoir," *Harvard Theological Review* 77 (1984) esp.
106.

For in this perspective ["(i)n Christ"] death has become an event in the communication of *life*, real and true life. And that is the meaning of death in the domain of Jesus." (Sermon 9, p. 85)

Maddening McGill

Maddening McGill. He can take us by the hand and lead us—and leave us. Or we leave him. Either way, he's off; and we are in the dust. Who leaves whom? McGill invites one to wonder where he is going. He is a master of rhetorical tease. "People say: God will resurrect us and will bring us back to life again. Let's hope not. Isn't 50-60-90 years of this life enough?" (Sermon 15, p. 127). "Who of you does not live amidst failures of love?" (Sermon 15, p. 129). McGill's disquieting honesty meets us early and often. One of McGill's most successful themes is *failure*—as in "failures of love." "Most of our love is resentment love" (Sermon 7, p. 71).[12] "Love is not our primary motive. Resentment is primary and we express this as—love" (Sermon 7, p. 71):

> Are we so filled with fear—fear of the hate that is in us, and fear of the hate that may be in other people—*that our love has no reality of its own?* . . . Thanksgivers, unless you let your God see the exaspera-tion and outrage that you feel at the negatives of life, unless you stop making thanksgiving a mask to hide despair and resentment, how is any movement toward authentic thanksgiving even possible? . . . Thanksgiving day should be a day of truth, love and anger, of anger making claims on love by being indignant about abuse and neglect; and of love making claims on anger by forgiveness. Thanksgiving Day should never become a lie of sweetness and light. (Sermon 7, pp. 69–70, 72–73; italics added)

Sounds like a recipe for a great Thanksgiving dinner. Family gatherings can be risky. McGill's sermon ("Be Angry") closes with a prayer preceded by these words: "Let us have a little more openness about our animosity. Then—and only then—can we begin to receive and exercise [receiving comes before exercising] our generosity" (Sermon 7, p. 73). "Truth is meant to save you first, and the comfort comes afterwards."

---

[12] James Breech grasps this: "This view of love which tolerates everything and which does not see things as they are is rooted in the contemporary hatred of actuality, in *resentment*"—James Breech, *The Silence of Jesus: The Authentic Voice of the Historical Man* (Philadelphia: Fortress, 1983), 206. See 13–18. With the help of Max Scheler, Friedrich Nietzsche, and Fyodor Dos-toevsky, among others, this fine book is pervaded with McGillian perception, as Breech's "Ac-knowledgments" acknowledge (ix).

Related failure: in his sermon on "Loneliness," McGill advances the view that ". . . we try to build artificial bridges across the gap that separates us from one another, bridges made of such easy and faithless acts as the shaking of hands" (Sermon 1, p. 25). (Why should shaking hands be a faithless act?) "How we flee from God! How we seek to make a false god of our neighbor . . ." (Sermon 1, p. 25): the failure of "neighborolatry." Failure: "We, of ourselves, *do not worship God.* We cannot" (Sermon 12, p. 108). Rather, one steps into—or is caught up in—the worship of the Father by the Son. We participate. Now participation can be freeing, can be fun because freeing. I join in singing the chorus but am not (thank God) the guardian of the verse. The freedom to fail is also the freedom to succeed, and both freedoms are the freedom to *live*.

Consider McGill's investment in the *body*, the *flesh*:[13] "How do we arise? Out of an embrace of flesh, tangents of our father's pitiful lust, in midnight heat on dawnbed ease. The glory of our begetting was a twitch and gasp" (Sermon 13, p. 114).[14] And death? "And how do we end? Always through our body and with our bodies. . . . The body is our Achilles' heel" (Sermon 13, p. 114). "Every instant of life is therefore an advance of death" (Sermon 13, p. 114). "Death awaits us and death is total destitution" (Sermon 6, p. 61). Who leaves whom?

McGill speaks of "the deep suffering that belongs to our daily life" (Sermon 2, p. 30). Or, in the understated irony of Søren Kierkegaard's humoristic-philosophical pseudonym, Johannes Climacus, "To be in existence is always a bit inconvenient."[15] Indeed. Next, McGill calls us to the lifelong "work and a constant learning" of coming ". . . to know our own suffering . . ." (Sermon 2, p. 30). Who leaves whom? Regarding the idea of a God who is good to us by helping us live in this world: "For everything that God gives us does not really give us life: it only fattens us for death" (Sermon 12, p. 107). Who leaves whom? "Why aren't we furious at God and exasperated for

---

[13] See *The Celebration of Flesh.*

[14] McGill invites us to "[c]onsider our attitude toward romantic love. According to the popular songs [do they render "our" attitude?], the final truth about love is that it will leave us. However real it may be now, the day will come when we will 'wonder who's kissing her now . . .' . . ." See McGill, "Reason in a Violent World" in Wesleyan University Alumni-Faculty Seminar, *The Distrust of Reason* (Middletown, CT: Wesleyan University, June, 1959), 43.

[15] Johannes Climacus (Søren Kierkegaard), *Concluding Unscientific Postscript to* Philosophical Fragments, I, ed. and trans. Howard V. Hong and Edna H. Hong (Princeton: Princeton University Press, 1992), 452, Kierkegaard's Writings, XII.1, translation altered. The Hongs translate, "To be in existence is always somewhat troublesome . . ." See also Johannes Climacus (Søren Kierkegaard), *Concluding Unscientific Postscript*, trans. David F. Swenson and Walter Lowrie (Princeton: Princeton University Press, 1941), 404: "For to be in existence is always a somewhat embarrassing situation . . .").

the wretchedness of so many humans? That wouldn't be nice" (Sermon 7, p. 69). If we have not left him, McGill prepares us to receive the wisdom in the recognition of C. FitzSimons Allison, ". . . we worship God by expressing our honest anger at him."[16]

The Recognizable and the Revolutionary

"Ah, Ah!" writes—exclaims—McGill (Sermon 10, p. 93). "Ah, Ah!"—explicitly or unspoken—is at the center of McGill's sermons; and the exclamation point is for us. Nearby are "Well!" (Sermon 17, p. 145) and "Exactly" (Sermon 3, p. 38; Sermon 17, p. 145). McGill leads us on and draws us in. He is an intellectual seducer. The "irascibility" can cloak a certain playfulness which now and then peeks through.[17]

McGill often begins with some form of push away from presumed expectations.[18] He did not want to be "the expected," and he was not. In listening to or in reading McGill, one comes to wonder, "Just where is he going?" because one can seldom be sure—or safely anticipate. Conversely, McGill likes to begin with the recognizable. Then comes the "revolution" sparked by such characteristic and apparently calm words as "Let us now look at the New Testament . . ." (Sermon 3, p. 34). Or: "All this sounds fine provided we do not look too closely at the New Testament witness to Jesus" (Sermon 10, p. 94). Here we go again. Just when we think we see at last where McGill is going and suppose he has arrived there, he changes direction and takes a turn to a new course, an instinctive theological quarterback. Thus, "We have missed the heart of the story" (Sermon 17, p. 145). McGill revels in offense. He is relentless. He is full of surprises—"Some Real Surprises"—and obviously enjoys being so. "Now begins your preparation for the vocation of dying" (Sermon 6, p. 62). When is the last time we heard that in a commencement address? Or: "Philanthropy is a typically evil form of love" (Sermon 14, p. 120). *What? Philanthropy?* "Philanthropy," as McGill treats it, is near the top of his hate list because "giving becomes grounded on having and becomes

[16] C. FitzSimons Allison, *Guilt, Anger, and God: The Patterns of Our Discontents* (New York: Seabury, 1972), 88.

[17] See Cain, "Arthur McGill: A Memoir," 100–101.

[18] For example, "At the present moment [ca. 1975] witchcraft and Satanism are enjoying a mild popularity in the United States. It seems to me that these are simply faddish archaisms, and as such they will not concern me here," "Structures of Inhumanity" in Alan M. Olson, ed., *Disguises of the Demonic: Contemporary Perspectives on the Power of Evil* (New York: Association, 1975), 116. Or: "Let me begin with some preliminary remarks which will indicate certain directions that I will not follow," "Human Suffering and the Passion of Christ" in Flavian Dougherty, CP, ed., *The Meaning of Human Suffering* (New York: Human Sciences, 1982), 159.

an expression of having" (Sermon 14, p. 120). If philanthropy is out, what is next on the McGillian hit list? "Humanism": "Humanism is another form of resentment love" (Sermon 7, p. 72). Then comes the about-face, the McGillian "flip": "Do not ask, how can we who love also hope? Rather ask, how can we who love do anything but hope? How can we love for one moment without finding ourselves hoping for the kingdom of God?" (Sermon 15, p. 129). The bite here is harsh appraisal of present life as incentive for Christian hope; while, at the same time, "gratitude" is aligned with "life" and a powerful authorization of vulnerability. Christianity authorizes vulnerability because the Christian God authorizes vulnerability—because the Christian God *is* vulnerability. McGill comments on and warns against—

> . . . the effort to worship an unneedy and invulnerable God. If such a God indeed excludes every possibility of needy brokenness, this God also excludes the life actualized in Jesus. For this God is not the creator of shared life but simply a product of the human outrage at evil. (Sermon 5, p. 51)

Crucial (literally) to McGill's Christian theology is the recognition that ". . . neediness belongs properly and naturally to God" (Sermon 5, p. 51)— and hence (via *imago dei*) to us. Manifestation of our neediness informs the life of faith:

> It might be said that those who cling to the past act of Jesus's resurrection and those who seek a flight into heaven want too much here and now. They dislike the poverty, the religious poverty and ambiguity into which the ascension envelops us. They want to stand beyond uncertainty. But that is not possible. (Sermon 14, p. 122)

If one is looking for "relevance," here relevance is—in McGill's rejection of our yearning "to stand beyond uncertainty" in matters of faith:

> The Christian cannot really separate himself in that way [standing beyond uncertainty or, as McGill soon goes on to say, standing with those who ". . . surpass the condition of perplexity and tension" (Sermon 14, p. 123)] from the gentile, from the polytheist who looks into his own concrete existence and sees a welter of principalities and powers [McGill has just been referring to Romans 8], sees a whole pantheon of gods manifesting their glory in his flesh and spirit—the power of war, the power of society, the power of sexuality, the power of disease—these flash their immensity in turn [note the alliance of gods and powers]. (Sermon 14, p. 122).

At times a brusque, even cryptic, writing complements a teasing and goading which pay off, challenging us to challenge ourselves with the possibility of a new way of seeing. McGill leaves us wondering, wanting to know more, newly convinced that there is more to be seen and said. And there is.

Setting the Stage for Scripture

When was the last time we heard a good sermon? What is a "good sermon"? McGill has some thoughts about this—but not much optimism:

> There is no reserve, no awe in the use of words in the churches. No words are holy, pregnant with energies that might shatter our existence. . . . Speech in the church is never dark, never in riddles. You hear sermons through the weeks and months and years, and they are no different in their basic rhetoric from a classroom lecture or a radio address. Can such sermons really serve as the center for a weekly religious celebration? Do they release such power that the act of delivering them must be surrounded and set apart by a liturgical service [or must they be surrounded and set apart precisely because of their impotence?]? (Sermon 10, p. 88)

How might persons have exited worship services after hearing a McGill sermon? Puzzled? Confused? Bewildered? Rarely "upbeat"? Rarely "sent out singing"? But surely McGill sent them out *thinking*—and us with them. Reading—hearing—McGill can be like walking the edge of an escarpment. Or listening to McGill can seem disheartening, discouraging, glum. "Don't we have trouble enough?" But in his determined, intrepid dialectic of perspectives, McGill can grab us and angle us into a startlingly, jarringly fresh way of seeing the same old biblical texts. Adventure ensues: "So *that's* what's going on!" The Bible: read it again for the first time—with Arthur McGill. The insights can be stunning.

McGill's sermons are neither simple nor easy to follow. Twists and turns and surprise departures are frequent. "How does that follow?" and "How did we get here?" are all about these sermons, which were surely delivered with pace, pause, deliberation and acceleration—with timing, helping to insinuate meanings and sub-meanings. On occasion was there a hint of a self-satisfied grin?

Thus, McGill delights in engaging perspectives, enlivening them, apparently entering into them and then blasting them, exposing them as outrageously untenable, obviously existentially inadequate. But the inadequacy was not so obvious a sentence ago. Often the lost, futile perspectives are attributed to us and to our day, to contemporaneity, to the United States. In "Jonah and Human Grandeur," McGill refers to:

> God's call to Jonah: "Go to the great city of Nineveh and denounce it for its wickedness" [Jonah 1:2] . . . We must remember this: the wick-

edness of Nineveh—alas!—is the wickedness of the United States,
and the oppressiveness of Nineveh appears also in the United States.
(Sermon 4, p. 46)

(Is something of William Stringfellow lurking alongside McGill?[19])

We encounter in McGill the ability to present a bold, brash engendering
of perspectives and to set perspectives in opposition. Frequently the perspective developed becomes a foil for a perspective enjoined, which is often not
"developed" but alluded to, hinted at, pointed toward.[20] We find the relentless redoing of a distinct perspective, often a perspective that is a surprise to
us, that takes us by surprise, disorienting and disarming us. At the same time,
McGill is able to evoke a familiar, all-too-familiar perspective and then to
gesture toward a counter-perspective powerfully, vividly, shatteringly. He can
plop a puzzling scriptural text down in that context and allow us suddenly
to see the logic of it. He places it deftly where it can come alive. He need not
interpret it. The perspective he has drawn does that.[21] All he has to do is to
watch us "get it":

> Blessed are the poor, the sorrowful, the hungry and the persecuted.
> These statements attributed to Jesus seem confused, if not nonsensi-
> cal . . .

[19] Stringfellow is working with the book of Revelation: "If America *is* Babylon, and Babylon
is *not* Jerusalem—confounding what, all along, so many Americans have been told or taught
and have believed—is there any American hope?

"The categorical answer is *no*." William Stringfellow, *An Ethic for Christians and Other
Aliens in a Strange Land* (1973; reprinted, Eugene, OR: Wipf & Stock, 2004), 155.

After including this reference, I found among McGill's papers (474 file folders of mainly
handwritten notes and manuscripts—McGill liked pencil, note cards held together with paper
clips, and any size sheet of paper at hand), a folder (#200) identified in McGill's hand as "Demonic: Misc notes." Rather than miscellaneous notes, the folder contains but one reference on
a 5" x 8" sheet: "On demonic principalities Stringfellow, An Ethic for Xians & Other Aliens
in a Strange Land [no underlining of title] 1973."

[20] Characteristically, the perspective at which we might wish to get a closer look "breaks away"
from the text. The tease again. McGill leaves us wanting more, but this is also an invitation
for us to do some work. For an analogy, see David Cain, "Notes on a Coach Horn: 'Going Further,' 'Revocation,' and *Repetition*" in Robert L. Perkins, ed., *Fear and Trembling* and
Repetition (Macon, GA: Mercer University Press, 1993), 341–42 (International Kierkegaard
Commentary, 6).

[21] Is this "perspective" language finally too tame? Is injustice done to the boldness, the radical-
ity of McGill? Finally, he is not proposing one perspective rather than another but pointing:
open your senses and hear, touch, smell, taste, see. By "perspective," I mean way of entertain-
ing (I almost wrote "seeing," but McGill wants all senses; see *The Celebration of Flesh*, 22–23),
not what McGill denounces as "viewpoint Christianity" (see *Celebration*, 13–14, 187–90, p.
2 above, and n. 26 below). I am grateful to William F. May for calling my attention to this
matter—and to others.

What Jesus's beatitudes do is to make clear the indispensable condition for receiving. We cannot receive unless we lack, unless we are in need. . . .

In other words, if you are not willing to be one with your neediness, you cannot be blessed. (Sermon 2, pp. 27–28)

After setting the stage for scripture, McGill concludes a sermon ("On Worship"): "Let me read again the lesson from Paul's letter to the Colossians" (Sermon 12, p. 109).

The Wind in the Tree

McGill affirms, "A technical language certainly has its place in the Christian community."[22] This warning follows:

whenever such technical language becomes an end in itself and is taken as the only true language in the church, whenever sermons and prayers are content to repeat theologically precise abstractions, then Christians are saying that their true life with God separates them from the *present concrete world*, and from the everyday speech that belongs to that world.[23]

In his sermon "Loneliness," McGill rehearses a story (one he thinks we might know, so this is not a story originating with him) of a child who hears the wind in a backyard tree. The tree becomes a mystery, alive—and special. The tree is later blown over in a storm. The child's parents do not understand: there are other trees. The child is alone—without the wind in *the* tree.

Specificity matters. In Federico Fellini's *La Strada*, a nighttime metaphysical[24] exchange occurs. Gelsomina (Giulietta Masina) hears Matto, "The Fool," (Richard Basehart) call her name. The conversation which follows is a mesmerizing moment in film:

The Fool: "Gelsomina." . . . What a funny face you have! Sure you're a woman? Not an artichoke? . . .

Gelsomina: . . . I'm no good to anybody . . . and I'm tired of living . . .

The Fool: You like to make love? What *do* you like? Gosh, but you're homely. . . .

Gelsomina: What am I here for on this earth? . . .

---

[22] *The Celebration of Flesh*, 36.

[23] Ibid., italics added.

[24] A whisper of redundancy . . .

The Fool: A book I once read said everything in this world serves a purpose . . . Take that stone, for instance . . .

Gelsomina: Which one?

The Fool: Anyone . . . even this one serves for something . . . or this one . . .

Gelsomina: For what?

The Fool: How should I know? . . . Know who I'd have to be? God! *He* knows everything! When you're born . . . when you die . . . Who else can know it? I don't know what this stone's good for, but it must serve something. Because if it's useless, *everything's* useless! Even the stars and even you! Even *you* serve some purpose with that homely artichoke head of yours.[25]

The Fool gives Gelsomina the particular stone he has picked up in illustrating his reflection. Gelsomina accepts the stone, attends to it carefully, caringly, nods, and beams with a new-found promise of purpose. The magic line: "Which one?" Which one? The tree blown over, the tree with wind no more.

Specificity matters:[26] "Love of all mankind, love for the human race. That's silly. Love is specific" (Sermon 7, p. 71). McGill is thinking of

---

[25] Screenplay, Federico Fellini, Tullio Pinelli, with Ennio Flaiano, *La Strada*, 1954. I am transcribing these words from a soundtrack, so the punctuation—and italics—are mine.

[26] McGill labeled file folder #188 "Concrete." Inside are seven 8½" x 11" lined sheets (but eight pages—the first sheet contains writing on both sides—and all but the last sheet are numbered) with one 5⅜" x 8½" sheet originally paper-clipped to page 7. The heading is "The Concrete." Here are a few suggestive excerpts: "Cultural difference, ie. differences in what people in different cultures think & see, are really determined by concrete features of their environment; they are not just developments coming out of internal collective history. Cf Wallace Stevens on exchanging person in [?] African jungle with [?], on meaning of sounds, on whole imaginative apperception. One source of cultural relativism is fact that the concrete impact of sensory exper[ience] is left out of view: culture is looked at too *wld* [world]-viewishly, too generally, too internally. The dynamic of life wrestling *constantly* with the *concrete as such* is neglected. Why? A common assumption that the concrete is wrestled with only derivatively & secondarily; the real wrestle is with whole wld. *Here is fund*[amental] *princ*[iple] *for me*: to locate human venture not at level of whole wld or God . . . but at level of wrestling with the concrete. That is where the creative edge of human exs [existence] always is. Hence primacy of phenomenology. . . . What ethics are involved in this attention to the concrete? . . . Here's where ethical impact of eschatology on relations to the concrete comes into play.

"The focus on the concrete means that art has a fundamental & indispensable role. . . . Art finds a form to recover the concrete as we newly & freshly experience it. Cf *Celebration of Flesh* Chap. 1.

"But obviously, to make a case for the centrality of the concrete for theology, I must be able to translate the basic & obvious theological categories—sin, salvation, judgment & grace, God, JX [Jesus Christ]—immediately into concrete experiences. That 'immediately' is crucial. . . .

the words of Ivan Karamazov to his younger brother, Alyosha, in Fyodor Dostoevsky's *The Brothers Karamazov*, which he knew well: [27]

> I could never understand how one can love one's neighbours. It's just one's neighbours, to my mind, that one can't love, though one might love those at a distance. . . . For any one to love a man, he must be hidden, for as soon as he shows his face, love is gone.[28]

Again the words which seem so right for McGill's dialectic: "Truth is meant to save you first, and the comfort comes afterwards." But there *is* an "afterwards"; and, in the sense that this "afterwards" is *grace*, in the sense that—in a different but related orchestration of McGill's dialectic—*receiving precedes giving*, this "afterwards" is "*before*":

> But there is something in God for my loneliness greater even than His knowledge or His justice. For in God I know not only that I am truly known, and by this knowledge truly judged, but that I am *understood*. . . . For the person of the Son Himself became flesh like us, suffering in Himself every agony the human soul can encounter. Therefore He who knows every hypocrisy and evil in our thoughts, knows these from our point of view. And He also knows the secret beauty of the nature He gave us. He knows the deep recesses of goodness in us of which we ourselves have not the slightest knowledge.

"The concrete exper[ience] is not self-enclosed [or *need not be* self-enclosed; this is one of the grand intimations—and realizations of art: tapped in certain ways, the concrete can touch the universal] . . .

"Does Ritual belong to the concrete exper or not? . . .

"How is naiveté related to concrete experience? Naiveté is the acceptance of concrete experience . . .

"Concrete exper[ience] has an appalling inadequacy about it. Eliot 'Portrait of Lady' 'Gerontion' Eliot identifies this with transiency. The theoretical way is a response to this inadequacy. But it is a false response. Question: Does JX [Jesus Christ] give us another focus *away from* concreteness, involving renunciation of the world? Cf Eliot 'Ash Wednesday.' Or does he establish us in a relation to God that requires concreteness, in its inadequacy? Humility, acceptance of our littleness & transiency. Does the inadequacy of concreteness direct us elsewhere in JX? Or is it to be accepted in JX by virtue of letting God be our glory?" As often in McGill, "inadequacy" is the way to the adequate—or to the more than adequate.

[27] McGill says much when he writes in his "Confession of Faith," ". . . I came through readings in American literature [with a little Russian literature on the side], curiously enough [or not], to the shattering apprehension of the reality of God . . ."—see below, p. 148. Literature implicates specificity. See the reference to literature again, p. 154. In this statement, McGill writes also of "the positive acceptance of the other person . . ." (p. 152). This, again, is specificity. Appropriately enough, much in this "Confession" helps to prepare one for the sermons. The sermons help to explicate the "Confession."

[28] Fyodor Dostoyevsky, *The Brothers Karamazov*, trans. Constance Garnett (New York: Random House, 1950) 281. James Breech quotes and comments on this passage in *The Silence of Jesus*, 18.

> Also God's knowledge of us is a loving knowledge . . . which cre-
> ates in us the goodness we do not have alone. . . . God's knowledge
> saves and redeems us, so that if once you know that you are truly
> known to God, you not only experience justice, but you also experi-
> ence mercy and redemption. (Sermon 1, p. 26)

McGill exacerbates (or so we might wish to believe) the negative. One must look and listen carefully for a bleep, a pinch of the positive. But it is there—or implied. This is a note not often sounded, and yet McGill is empty without it. It is a grace note.[29] I recall hearing McGill conclude a lecture on *agape* in Seipp Alcove, Firestone Library, Princeton University, by quoting a little verse of Abner Dean titled "Grace Note":

> Remember the word—?
> The one from the manger—?
> It means only this . . .
> You can dance
> with a stranger.[30]

"Grace Note": as in music, as in faith.

How near McGill's dialectical words are to those of Barth, words he may not have known directly but words which he might have accounted for in the words of Barth reported by William Stringfellow, "We read the same Bible . . . ."[31]

> "Eternal life" is not another, second life beyond our present one, but
> the reverse side of this life, as God sees it, which is hidden from us
> here and now. It is this life in relationship to what God has done in
> Jesus Christ for the whole world and thus also for us. So we wait and
> hope—in respect of our death—to be made manifest with him (Jesus
> Christ who is raised from the dead), in the glory of judgment, and
> also in the grace of God. That will be the new thing: that the veil

---

[29] McGill affirms, "Victory . . . is the decisive and final fact of human existence"— "Reason in a Violent World," 47.

[30] Abner Dean, *Wake Me When It's Over* (New York: Simon & Schuster, 1955) 59.

[31] Stringfellow gives this account: "I raised with Karl Barth during his visit [to the United States, 1962] the matter which is basic here. Again and again, in both the public dialogue and in our private conversations, it had been my experience that as Barth began to make some point, I would at once know what he was going to say. It was not some intuitive thing, it differed from that, it was a recognition, in my mind, of something familiar that Barth was articulating. When this had happened a great many times while I listened to him, I described my experience to him and asked why this would happen. His response was instantaneous: 'How could it be otherwise? We read the same Bible, don't we?'"—William Stringfellow, *A Second Birthday* (1970; reprinted, Eugene, Oregon: Wipf & Stock, 2005) 151–52. Hermeneutics! The point must be: we read the same Bible because we read the Bible *in the same way*.

which now lies over the whole world and thus over our life (tears, death, sorrow, crying, grief) will be taken away, and God's counsel (already accomplished in Jesus Christ) will stand before our eyes, *the object of our deepest shame, but also of our joyful thanks and praise.*[32]

Where is McGill going? He is going to side with the "enemy," in this case with our loneliness, and to turn the perspective so that the enemy may be seen in a new light as friend:

> The Lord God Almighty, He alone knows us, and our loneliness is like a goad by which He leads us to Himself. . . . You see that our loneliness from one another is not an evil to be overcome or a despair from which we try to escape, but is rather the sign within us which turns us to our true Lord, to Him who truly knows and judges and redeems. (Sermon 1, pp. 25–26)

In construing loneliness in this way, McGill has led us to the famous "prayer" at the beginning of Augustine's *Confessions*: "Yet man, this part of your creation, wishes to praise you. You arouse him to take joy in praising you, for you have made us for yourself, and our heart is restless until it rests in you."[33] So also is the witness of Arthur McGill.

The flash and flare, the fireworks, the dash and dare—the provocations—of McGill came through in classroom lectures and seminars vividly. In the words of the sermons which follow, glimpses, hints, intimations, the provocations—and theological fascinations—persist. Theological fascinations: Arthur McGill does not go haltingly, hesitantly, into theological-hermeneutical matters holding open some possibility of faith in a world so "come of age" that it begins to feel a bit aged. No limping. McGill is on the offensive, in more than one sense, as we have seen. He is aggressive. Any embarrassment of faith is an embarrassment of riches in which the paramount theme is becoming poor.

Ordering the Sermons

Presenting the following seventeen sermons of Arthur McGill in chronological order is not possible. The sermons bridge at least twenty-eight years, from 1951 to 1979. Sometimes we have specific dates, sometimes years. Sometimes we have place and no date, sometimes date and no place.

The sermons are arranged thematically; though this, too, is a challenge because the sermons return again and again to soon-familiar themes. Some

---

[32] Eberhard Busch, *Karl Barth: His Life from Letters and Autobiographical Texts,* trans. John Bowden (Philadelphia: Fortress, 1975), 488 (italics added).

[33] *The Confessions of St. Augustine,* trans. John K. Ryan (Garden City, NY: Doubleday, 1960), 43.

sermons could be placed with others according to one theme or grouped with yet others on the basis of another theme. (How many of these seventeen sermons treat of death? All of them, directly or indirectly; directly in most.) Nonetheless, four groupings suggest themselves.

I. Good Neediness

1. "Loneliness": Our loneliness is a goad to God.

2. "Beatitudes": Lack, need, receiving in gratitude, and life are identified.

3. "The Problem of Possessions": God's love sets poverty in a new light: love is not minding being poor.

4. "Jonah and Human Grandeur": Hunger for grandeur yields oppression; acceptance of failure yields freedom.

5. "Suffering": Neediness belongs to God.

6. "Needed—An Education in Poverty": Commencement is a time to own the vocation of dying.

II. Kinds of Power, Love, and Death

7. "Be Angry": Dare to face truth, love—and anger at God first of all.

8. "Palm Sunday Sermon": Jesus is not a victim but agent of death as self-expenditure bearing the fruit of life.

9. "Eucharist": The meaning of death in the domain of Jesus is the communication of life.

10. "Harvard Convocation": Proper speech is the deed of self-expenditure.

11. "Tower Hill Graduation—Against the Expert": Make your actions, suffering—and your death—your own.

12. "On Worship": We participate in the worship of the Father by the Son.

III. Qualitative Hope

13. "The Centrality of Flesh": Look out Lent: Christianity is a festival of flesh.

14. "The Ascension": In uncertainty, risk measuring the meaning of letting go by the power of Christ and not by the power of death.

15. "The Goal of Our History": Hope not in the future but in God.

IV. Grace

16. "Jesus and the Myth of Neighborliness": The good Samaritan is Jesus Christ.

17. "The Good Samaritan": The good Samaritan is Jesus Christ.

Perhaps these last overlapping, complementary sermons are appropriately placed together in a section on "Grace." As suggested, grace may seem to be a "Grace Note"; but it motivates the whole of McGill's theology. McGill's treatment of the good Samaritan (Luke 10:25–37) as our neighbor so that we can "Go and do likewise" (Luke 10:37) not out of our own power, our surplus, our "philanthropy," but out of God's gracious giving—"We love because God first loved us" (1 John 4:19); receiving precedes giving—may be regarded as McGill's central theological theme.[34]

■ ■ ■

Editorial Note

I am most grateful to Lucy McGill for entrusting to me, on the recommendation of William F. May and Paul Ramsey, the papers of Arthur McGill so long ago, for her transcription of sermon manuscripts—and for her patience; to William F. May for his role in granting me "the McGill files," for his patience and encouragement, and for graciously contributing a "Foreword" to this collection; to Paul Ramsey for his caring and kindness; to Chuck Balestri and Egbert Giles Leigh, Jr., friends since Princeton undergraduate days (some forty-six years); to Chuck for so many rewarding McGill-catalytic or McGill-catalyzed conversations at Princeton, 1960–1963, when we were both under McGill's spell; to Egbert, Biologist at the Smithsonian Tropical Research Institute, Barro Colorado Island, Panama, for his enduring interest and encouragement; to Cindy Toomey, Administrative and Program Specialist, Department of Classics, Philosophy, and Religion (CPR), University of Mary Washington, who has indeed been a "specialist" in sundry ways; to JeanAnn Dabb, Associate Professor of Art and Art History, UMW, for introducing me to ARTstor; and to Wipf and Stock Publishers and Ted Lewis, Jim Tedrick, K. C. Hanson, Heather Carraher, and associates for their investment in Arthur McGill.

When Arthur McGill penciled, often rapidly—one can see the acceleration of the writing in his hand—a vast paper trail of theological fascinations,

---

[34] See McGill, *Suffering: A Test of Theological Method* (Philadelphia: Westminster, 1982), 99–111; chapter 6, "Resting in Our Need."

he did not know that persons someday would struggle to decipher his difficult and often minuscule hand. He was about his own present, pressing, and remarkable intellectual adventures. Still, the paper clips attaching little sheets to larger sheets to note cards in sometimes thick and puzzling disarray are thwarting. And the abbreviations . . .

The concern here is to respect the text. "Man" and "he" and "him" are untouched. Commas and semi-colons posed a temptation: add some, subtract others. With rare exceptions, punctuation-wise, spelling-wise, capitalization-wise and otherwise (and apart from possible misreadings of the manuscripts), the texts have been permitted to stand. When manuscript baffles or temptations triumph, there are brackets [ ]—different kinds and a "non-kind": 1) [word?] means this is an uncertain but best-guess reading; 2) [?] means there is a word, but I haven't a clue; 3) [??] means more than one indecipherable word; 4) no brackets means either no need for brackets or that possibly there were brackets which have been removed because the reading is likely and because the reader needs to be spared endless, distracting brackets. When the manuscripts become outline or word-notes, I have risked making coherent connections, again within brackets. Originally, every added "a," "the," "we," "our" and infrequently added punctuation mark was dutifully placed in brackets. Brackets, brackets everywhere. I decided to do away with the brackets in the case of articles, etc., but retain them in the case of other additions. There are too many brackets, and every set of brackets is (for now)[35] a defeat. References given by McGill are in parentheses. Added references are in brackets. Often the manuscripts slip into "inverse paragraphs": instead of indentation of the first line, lines under the first line are indented. This accounts in part for many of the short—and one-sentence—paragraphs; though at times I have created paragraphs. Then there are the dreaded outlines and infinitesimal marginal notes.

McGill uses different translations of scripture, the King James Version (identified in the text as KJV), the Revised Standard Version (RSV), and, quite often, The New English Bible (NEB). Sometimes there seems to be no exact fit, and no translation is designated. The version may well be MM = McGill's Memory. When a text is indicated but not quoted by McGill, the RSV is used—unless McGill's words operate off of another translation.

David Cain
University of Mary Washington

---

[35] Often I have stared at a word with magnifying glass for extended times over days—and over years. Then, suddenly, the word is clear and unmistakable: no brackets of any kind. A little victory. Lucy McGill has been responsible for many such victories.

I

Good Neediness

*"If you are not willing to be one with your neediness,
you cannot be blessed."*

—Sermon 2

Loneliness

Sermon submitted in Candidacy for Licensure
October 28, 1951

*I looked on my right hand,
and beheld, but there was no
man that would know me.
No man cared for my soul.
(Psalm 142:4, KJV)*[1]

We have all at one time or another, when we joined with an unfamiliar group of people, felt strangely alone. All of the time, I suppose, we are vaguely uneasy because no one quite understands us. We are always pushed by a subtle insecurity in an effort to show ourselves to our neighbor, to bridge the gap of ignorance and indifference between us. But at a party where no face is known, or in a new town to which we have just moved, we experience this insecurity and fear of loneliness in a peculiarly acute way.

On the other hand, when we go back to our parents' house for Thanksgiving or Christmas dinner, we feel a wonderful reassurance because this loneliness is almost conquered. All the objects in the family home—the pictures on the wall, the designs in the rugs—are part of our own intimate past. To the people around us we are closely bound by the memory of experiences which we went through together. We love to tell the old jokes, to rehearse past events. Here we have a peculiar sense of belonging; here we seem to be known and accepted by others; here for a moment we seem not to be isolated, but together.

In the ancient world, the family was given tremendous importance in a man's life, because there was here an understanding, a familiarity, and a loyalty among the members which made it a unique *spiritual* community. Here

---

[1] Punctuation is altered, and a phrase is omitted.

a man sank the roots of himself, here he was not alone. But in our day the family no longer has this meaning for children or for parents. We still have the custom of letting male children keep the family name. But the family is not consciously thought of and honored and defended as the place—the one place—where we are not alone, the place where others are loyal—truly loyal—to us, and we respond with loyalty to them, the place where we commit to others certain usually hidden parts of our personality. The family is not consciously valued in this way anymore. It is not appreciated or used by our souls. We have lost the ability to tap the spiritual resources which family intimacy offers. The liberal divorce laws and the automobile by no means *caused* the breakup of the family. They were merely occasions where our new inner attitude became visible in action.

Lacking the unique spiritual community of a family, you and I today are especially burdened with loneliness. Too often even the Thanksgiving dinners and birthday parties are not thought of as *expressions* of a real conscious sense of being together. Too often they are nothing but artificial attempts to escape from loneliness, attempts to fabricate a community which we wish existed but do not really experience as there in actuality. At the family reunions we avoid talking about the deep personal realities with which we struggle. We talk about the trivial things or about the irrelevant parts of the past. How many veterans come home and feel that it is utterly impossible for their parents to have the least understanding of their spiritual struggles. It was not always like this. In former times the father was the one to whom a son could communicate and share his spiritual problems. But today, even in the family, we feel cut off at the deepest springs of life.

Every person learns the awful fact of this loneliness very early in life. Perhaps you know the short story about the little child who one day hears the wind in one of the trees in his backyard. The tree acquires for the child a mystery, an aliveness, and becomes very special for the child. Then that tree is blown over in a storm; the child is bewildered and hurt and frightened. But when he comes to his parents and asks why *that* tree was destroyed, what can they understand? So they smile at the strangeness of children and explain how many other trees there are in the backyard. The child finds that his inner bewilderment is not understood—somehow he is alone with it.

Everyday experience is full of incidents that starkly reveal the gap which separates us from one another. Take something as common as pain. One might think that because many have endured pain, we should understand each other's agony. But the very opposite is true. No one can understand how your physical pain fits into the complex hopes and fears and frustration which torment your soul. This is the part of pain which needs understanding and encouragement, yet this is the very part where we are alone.

I find hospital calls to be the most difficult part of the ministry. What do *you* say to your sick friend? You may show the furrowed brow of deep sympathy and concern. This may be all right, but it is not enough. It does not clarify or strengthen the sufferer in his inner struggles. If anything seeing the grave expression on your face only intensifies his bewilderment and frustration and feeling of hopelessness. Or, instead, you may visit your sick friend with jokes and gaity, trying to cheer him up. This may also be good, but it too is not enough. You do not touch the trouble and despair that is perplexing his soul. The smile you give him is just on his lips; you do not put laughter in his heart. The loneliness of pain makes us think of the suffering of Job, his anguish at the injustice of it, and the utter failure of others to understand his indignation.

How we want to run from the terrible pressure of this loneliness! We like to hear voices near us—the radio, the telephone. We do not ask that they say anything to us, but we plead with them to distract us from our sense of being alone. We join clubs and chat about trivial external matters like the weather and sports. We sniff about for causes in the service to which we hope to be united with others. We have a gentleman's agreement with each other. I agree to appear happy when I see you, to ask after your health, to seem concerned over your problems and amused at your jokes if—*if* you will do the same for me. So we try to build artificial bridges across the gap that separates us from one another, bridges made of such easy and faithless acts as the shaking of hands.

How we flee from God! How we seek to make a false god of our neighbor, a god who will flatter us and do our will! How we seek the applause and love of men, hoping to find security and salvation in their approving eyes!

The Lord God Almighty, He alone knows us, and our loneliness is like a goad by which He leads us to Himself.

> I looked about me but there was no man who would bother
> to know me. All refuge failed me; I had nowhere to turn . . .
> But I poured out my suffering before the Lord; I showed Him my trouble.
> (Psalm 142:4, 2; no translation match found)

For men can only know us from the outside, on the basis of appearances. God alone knows us from the inside. He made us as we are, and only He knows us as we are—knows us as we do not even know ourselves.

That is why there is no justice among men. How can any man judge you justly if he has no knowledge of you from the inside? To be known by other people is to be unjustly known—it is to be alone in the deepest sense of the word. For whether people praise you or condemn you, they do so ignorantly and unjustly. Therefore, when Jesus stood before Pilate, before the human

judge, and was commanded to defend himself, he owed it to himself to remain silent [see John 18:33—19:16]. No matter what he would have said,
men could not have understood him justly, any more than a jury can know
the heart and truth of the men whom they must judge. Because only God
knows us, only He can render us justice; without God, your existence and
mine would be immersed in the injustice of what other people think of us,
and the injustice of our opinion of ourselves. We would be helpless victims
of the ignorant flattery and ignorant condemnation from others and from
ourselves without truth or hope.

But there is something in God for my loneliness greater even than His
knowledge or His justice. For in God I know not only that I am truly known,
and by this knowledge truly judged, but that I am *understood*. Even though
God condemns me, I know that he understands me. For the person of the
Son Himself became flesh like us, suffering in Himself every agony the human soul can encounter. Therefore He who knows every hypocrisy and evil
in our thoughts, knows these from our point of view. And He also knows the
secret beauty of the nature He gave us. He knows the deep recesses of goodness in us of which we ourselves have not the slightest knowledge.

Also God's knowledge of us is a loving knowledge—a knowledge which
does not judge us from a distance but which also understands our inner
struggles from our own viewpoint, and which creates in us the goodness we
do not have alone. God's knowledge saves and redeems us, so that if once you
know that you are truly known to God, you not only experience justice, but
you also experience mercy and redemption. You see that our loneliness from
one another is not an evil to be overcome or a despair from which we try to
escape, but is rather the sign within us which turns us to our true Lord, to
Him who truly knows and judges and redeems.

Beatitudes[1]

Seeing the crowds, he [Jesus] went up on the mountain, and when he sat down his disciples came to him. And he opened his mouth and taught them, saying:

"Blessed are the poor in spirit, for theirs is the kingdom of heaven.

Blessed are those who mourn, for they shall be comforted.

Blessed are the meek, for they shall inherit the earth.

Blessed are those who hunger and thirst for righteousness,
*   for they shall be satisfied.*

Blessed are the merciful, for they shall obtain mercy.

Blessed are the pure in heart, for they shall see God.

Blessed are the peacemakers, for they shall be called sons of God.

Blessed are those who are persecuted for righteousness' sake,
*   for theirs is the kingdom of heaven.*

Blessed are you when men revile you and persecute you and utter all kinds of evil against you falsely on my account. Rejoice and be glad, for your reward is great in heaven, for so men persecuted the prophets who were before you. . . ." [Matthew 5:1-12]

Blessed are the poor, the sorrowful, the hungry and the persecuted.

These statements attributed to Jesus seem confused, if not nonsensical, when we look at them by themselves. How can poverty or sorrow or hunger or

[1] The manuscript gives neither place nor date. Lucy McGill has sought to fill in probable dates, noting, "Dates which are not on the manuscripts have been supplied as approximate time of the delivery of the sermons by L. O. McGill." The suggested time of "Beatitudes" is 1975–1976. No scriptural text is included, but the sermon clearly depends on Matthew 5. The first twelve verses are included here.

persecution be the condition for blessedness, for beatitude, for perfect happiness?

The meaning of these beatitudes becomes a bit clearer when we remember the New Testament emphasis on love as giving and receiving. When churches address affluent people like us, they tend to talk about the importance of giving, of attending to the poor, the sick and the oppressed. The assumption always is that these teachings refer to other people whom we are called to help.

What churches have not made clear is that the primary human relation to love does not consist in giving but in receiving. In fact the New Testament is wholly preoccupied with God's loving the world that people may receive. Beatitude is to receive the fullness of life.

What Jesus's beatitudes do is to make clear the indispensable condition for receiving. We cannot receive unless we lack, unless we are in need. The need does not have to be excruciating, though it may be. But if we are to know the kind of love emphasized in the New Testament, the love that constantly gives nourishment and strength and order for a true life, we can only receive that gifted nourishment to the extent that we need it. Otherwise the gift will not touch us deeply, and receiving the gift will not arouse in us much gratitude or much life.

What Jesus's beatitudes say is simply this: Blessed are those who receive into the depths and center of themselves. And only those can receive into the depths and center of themselves who are impoverished there, or who are sorrowful there, or who are hungry there, or who are persecuted there.

In other words, if you are not willing to be one with your neediness, you cannot be blessed.

Now this opens a very deep problem in human nature: the problem of concealing and hiding our own suffering and neediness from ourselves. That is a fundamental human capacity, but it is fatal for those relationships and for that creativity which nourish need. In other words, it is fatal for the love that involves the communication of energy or strength or nourishment into need.

Let me give you an example. The poor of Brazil exist in a condition of such poverty and so much sickness that life for them should be an intolerable nightmare. As you may know, great efforts are are being made, not very successfully, to teach them literacy and to arouse them into revolutionary cadres.

What is so extraordinary among these people is the way in which they do not address their suffering. According to many accounts, what they do is to see their suffering as one of the given necessities in the nature of things. But for them that means that their suffering belongs to the cosmos. That is the character of external reality. It stands for them like a vast Himalayan immensity which tends to swallow them up.

As you can realize such a way of construing their situation means that their suffering does not really belong to their level of reality. There is suffering in them, but that which produces their suffering has, as it were, the fixed immensity of God. Not only does this make it absurd for them to do anything about their incredible suffering. This interpretation also has the effect of taking their suffering out of their own hands. They are not responsible for it. They themselves, as persons, have no creative role in relation to it. In exactly this way they deaden some of the outrage, some of the exasperation, some of the degradation involved in their suffering.

Let me turn from this realm of the world to our own lives for another example. American middle-class youth are taught to look for themselves, ahead of themselves, away from themselves. They are taught to locate their real being in what they will become, and they learn to lose themselves in this or that "interest," in this or that ambition, in this or that distraction. In fact, for many college students, if you deprive them of "interests" and diversions and at the same time if for a moment they stop projecting themselves into the future, they become very distressed.

How are these people trained to live in this way? How can people live out of touch with their specific present? I have come to the conclusion that there does not operate here simply the positive attraction of the future, or of this or that object of interest. There is also working in them a negative feeling of dislike for what they are now. It is not only that they want to be preoccupied with astronomy or to become a pianist. They also have come to feel dissatisfied or reproachful about themselves now. In other words, they carry in themselves a profound sense of their own present inadequacy. They are instilled with shame.

In one of its characteristics, shame involves the wish to hide an inadequacy which we may find in ourselves. For many middle-class young people in the United States, however, this shame applies, not to some specific act which they did, but to their sense of themselves. Unfortunately, when they get a job, when they reach the point for which they are now striving, this self-dissatisfaction does not go away. It is too deeply embedded. When they secure a position, they keep on climbing up the ladder, working always ahead of themselves, in the flight and shame over themselves. And for the rest of their lives, whenever the flight into interests or the future has to stop, they feel undone.

We cannot compare this suffering involved here with the agony of the South American poor. But here too we find operating a peculiar insensitivity to one's own suffering. For by living into an interest or into the future, these young people can keep their consciousness directed away from their unpleasing selves, and therefore they do not address, in fact, are hardly aware of the subtle suffering which they carry. This fear of failing may provide them with a sly reminder.

When Jesus relates a need and suffering to love, when he calls people into the life of love, this call is not a call for people to give love. It is also a call for people to receive love in connection with their suffering. Just at this point the power of the mind to hide our suffering from us comes into play. Because the mind is the greatest narcotic, it is extremely difficult for any of us to know our suffering, especially the deep suffering that belongs to our daily life. Therefore, to know our own suffering, much less to discover the meaning of love in connection with that suffering, involves a work and a constant learning the whole rest of our lives.

Possessions

Sermon delivered at the Congregational Church
Plainfield, New Jersey
January 16, 1966

For the word of the cross is folly to those who are perishing, but to us who are being saved it is the power of God. For it is written, "I will destroy the wisdom of the wise, and the cleverness of the clever I will thwart."

Where is the wise man? Where is the scribe? Where is the debater of this age? Has not God made foolish the wisdom of the world? For since in the wisdom of God, the world did not know God through wisdom, it pleased God through the folly of what we preach to save those who believe. For Jews demand signs and Greeks seek wisdom, but we preach Christ cruci-fied, a stumbling block to Jews and folly to Gentiles, but to those who are called, both Jews and Greeks, Christ the power of God and the wisdom of God. For the foolishness of God is wiser than men, and the weakness of God is stronger than men.

For consider your call, brethren; not many of you were wise according to worldly standards, not many were powerful, not many were of noble birth; but God chose what is foolish in the world to shame the wise, God chose what is weak in the world to shame the strong, God what is low and de-spised in the world, even things that are not, to bring to nothing things that are, so that no human being might boast in the presence of God. He is the source of your life in Christ Jesus, whom God made our wisdom, our righteousness and sanctification and redemption; therefore, as it is written, "Let him who boasts, boast of the Lord." (1 Corinthians 1:18–31)

For us in the United States, with our high standard of living, possessions absorb a good deal of our attention. We are always buying them, using them,

31

servicing them, replacing them and improving them. But this is no peculiarly American preoccupation. Not only the New Testament, but Jesus himself speaks repeatedly of wealth and poverty, and a good deal of the morality which our Lord teaches refers to this question of possessions.

I

Let us begin with our own experience. What are possessions to us? We must say two things: they are a great *burden* but a greater *blessing*. We can sum up their way of burdening us in two words: care and responsibilities.

Possessions of every kind are a care. There is the problem of securing and paying for them which in our credit-happy society can go on and on and on. There is the further problem of keeping them useful, keeping them in repair. The refrigerator refuses to work. The house needs another paint job. In the car motor there is an ominous plunk, plunk. Our possessions cause us so much care, so much worry and thought and time.

In addition, possessions are a serious responsibility. A person who has things cannot be indifferent to his neighbors. Whatever wealth he has imposes on him the task of using it well, not only for himself, but for his neighbors.

This is the basic law of every society, whether that of the pigmies of Africa or the ancient Chinese. An Indian has received his wealth from an environment and land, a situation which properly belongs to all the people of his tribe or nation. It is his private property only in a temporary and relative and minor sense. And if it means the preservation of the life of the people as a whole, his society will take his so-called property away from him without a moment's hesitation. The pigmy with his hut on a hill that is needed for observing possible enemy attacks loses his hut. The American businessman with his factory along the approved route of a superhighway loses his factory. The reason behind this practice is clear in every human society throughout history: in the last and final analysis, possessions are to help and nourish the common life in which each individual shares.

Therefore, a person with possessions not only feels care, he also feels responsibility. With his $50,000 house and three cars and swimming pool, he cannot be indifferent to the hungry and the destitute. His wealth imposes a special obligation on him. As we have found out from the experience of the peace corps, when rich parents do not feel this responsibility, their children do. And we know how the feeling of guilt over the way their families have been with their wealth has driven many a young man or woman into the peace corps.

These, then, are the burdens. Yet however severe they may be at times, everyone seems to agree that it is better to have possessions than not to have them. In other words, wealth is a blessing, and whatever anxieties and torments and responsibilities and guilt wealth may bring, at least it keeps us from a worse evil, the evil of poverty.

Behind the experience of all men with their possessions stands this fear of poverty. Why? Why are men afraid of it? The answer's obvious: frustration, fear and shame. To be poor means to be incapable of getting what you want. You don't have the means to realize your will, to achieve your values. Poverty means frustration, and it means all those diseases of the soul which arise from frustration—spite and envy against others who are more fortunate, self-pity towards oneself.

To be poor also means to be helpless in the face of threatening circumstances. It means to be unable to pay a taxi and get to work during a transit strike. It means to be unable to hire a lawyer to sue to recover damages from someone who has cheated you. It means to be unable to travel to Nevada for a divorce, or to Texas for that special heart operation needed to save your life. Poverty means fear, not momentary fear now and then, but the constant dread of knowing that there are no resources to fall back on, no financial cushion to claim the help of experts, knowing that with the least shift of circumstances you will go under and drown.

To be poor means, finally, to have nothing of benefit for others. It means not to be wanted or needed by other people. Who needs a poor man? Wherever he goes, he sees hostility and distress in the eyes of those who meet him. He begs from them, and they are confused, or sympathetic, or scornful. As long as he is not working, or at least trying to work, as long as he is not trying to be rich like everybody else, people put a wall between him and themselves. And he is utterly unable to do anything for them so as to claim their respect.

Poverty means shame, that dreadful shame which arises from a failure that cannot be concealed from others. These are the three dreadful faces of poverty: frustration, fear and shame. And whatever cares or responsibilities wealth may bring, to most people it seems like a picnic compared to poverty.

It can be said, therefore, that men love their possessions. But that is not really accurate. For it is not so much the positive goodness which lies in things that makes people cling to their possessions. It is rather the power of wealth to keep the evils of poverty away.

Wealth saves us—that is what we know. Therefore when we pray, O Lord, Deliver us from evil [Matthew 6:13], we probably mean, O Lord, give us the right possession to keep evil away. Give us money in the savings account when the accident occurs. Give us a fire extinguisher in the basement when the fire breaks out. Give us the right drug when our loved ones are sick.

O Lord, give us that which will deliver us from the evil and helplessness of being poor.

I have been speaking mainly of physical possessions. But all of this is even more true of spiritual possessions—of the virtue we may have or knowledge, or integrity, or vivacity. These, too, must be maintained with care and involve responsibilities. But these, too, keep us from an even more dreadful poverty than a lack of physical possessions.

II

Let us now look at the New Testament, to see what light it throws on the problem of possessions and poverty.

We can begin with the passage by Paul read as our morning lesson. Paul is speaking about the cross, about the fact that Christians celebrate Jesus's gruesome crucifixion as if it were a victory, an event of power and joy.

Paul observes that this makes no sense to the world, which cannot imagine why people should celebrate a death, and a death by being victimized.

"Where is the wise man? Where is the scribe? Where is the debater of this age? Has not God made foolish the wisdom of the world?" [1 Corinthians 1:20, RSV]. Human values and human wisdom simply collapse in the face of the horror and scandal of Jesus's death.

Paul's point is clear. The world judges everything according as it enhances man, or assists man, or improves man, or appreciates man. That is the wisdom of the world. And what are we confronted with in the cross of Jesus? No enhancement of man, no giving assistance to man, no improvement of man, no appreciation of man.

Do not imagine the cross as some kind of moral exercise by Jesus, where he exercises his virtues and displays his human goodness. Jesus died—he died all the way; he was not playing moral games. And because he died, it is impossible to look upon the cross as some new display of human possibility. And that, Paul says, is what shocks the world: that in the crucifixion, Christians should celebrate not Christ's virtue, not his forebearance on his enemies, not his courage, but his death, which shows that all these virtures went for nothing.

Then Paul turns to the people to whom he writes and reminds them that they, too, in their own experience repeat just what is found in the cross. "Not many of you were wise according to worldly standards, not many were powerful, not many were of noble birth" (1 Corinthians 1:26).[1] In short, not many were rich. "For," Paul continues,

---

[1] Again, McGill exercises some freedom with wording and punctuation. The RSV: "For consider your call, brethren; not many of you were wise according to worldly standards, not many were powerful, not many were of noble birth; . . ."

> God chose what is foolish in the world to shame the wise; God chose
> what is weak in the world to shame the strong; God chose what is low
> and despised in the world, even the things that are not, to bring to
> nothing the things that are, so that no human being might boast in
> the presence of God. (1 Corinthians 1:27–29, RSV)

Note carefully, Paul does not say, God shamed the wise and the strong and
the real[2] by giving his followers more wisdom, more strength and more reality, so that they could meet the world on its own terms and beat the world
all [hollow ?]. Just like the crucified Christ, the Christians were *and still are*
foolish and weak and, as it were, nothings in the world's terms. They were,
and they remain poor.

In this passage, of course, Paul is really elaborating a theme in Jesus's
own teaching. Here is the account from Mark 10:17–27:

> And as he was setting out on his journey, a man ran up and knelt
> before him, and asked him, "Good Teacher, what must I do to inherit
> eternal life?" And Jesus said to him, "Why do you call me good? No
> one is good but God alone. You know the commandments: 'Do not
> kill, Do not commit adultery, Do not steal, Do not bear false witness,
> Do not defraud, Honor your father and mother.'" And he said to him,
> "Teacher, all these I have observed from my youth." And Jesus look-
> ing upon him loved him, and said to him, "You lack one thing; go,
> sell what you have, and give to the poor, and you will have treasure
> in heaven; and come, follow me." At that saying his countenance fell,
> and he went away sorrowful; for he had great possessions.
>
> And Jesus looked around and said to his disciples, "How hard it
> will be for those who have riches to enter the kingdom of God!" And
> the disciples were amazed at his words. But Jesus said to them again,
> "Children, how hard it is to enter the kingdom of God! It is easier
> for a camel to go through the eye of a needle than for a rich man to
> enter the kingdom of God." And they were exceedingly astonished,
> and said to him, "Then who can be saved?" Jesus looked at them and
> said, "With men it is impossible, but not with God; for all things are
> possible with God." (RSV)

Jesus seems to be saying that wealth and possessions are simply no part
of a person sofar as he is related to God, and so far as he receives from God
eternal life. The wealthy [hypocrites] "already have their reward," he says in
another place (Matthew 6:2, 5, 16). In that form they will not receive the
blessings of God. Jesus did not here refer to selfish rich men or cruel rich men
or immoral rich men, simply to men who possess, and who need their possessions, who are afraid of being poor.

---

[2] "Real" seems to be surely the word written. And "reality" follows "wisdom" and "strength."
Perhaps "real" is coming from "the things that are." If so, "real" needs quotation marks.

We find the same point made by Jesus when he gives us the example of the child. For who is more unable to effect his own will than a child? Who is more helpless in the face of circumstances than a child? Who is more intimidated and made to feel shameful for his incompetence than a child?

The child is a figure of poverty, and that is why Jesus says: "Truly I say to you, unless you turn and become like children, you will never enter the kingdom of heaven. He is greatest in the kingdom of heaven who humbles himself like the child" (Matthew 18:3–4, RSV).[3] In the kingdom of God—at least of this God who sends Jesus—there is only poverty, and therefore only the humility which is happy in poverty.

The child of God does not cling to his possessions. He does not cling to his physical property. He does not cling to his spiritual wealth. He does not hold onto his own goodness, or his own knowledge. He is not good; he knows and sorrows for his sin. He is not knowledgeable; he is ignorant and rests in whatever knowledge his Lord has. He is not loving, filled with this peculiar power. He knows too well how little and feeble his love; he lives by the love of God in Jesus.

And when Jesus said, Blessed are the poor in spirit, he meant just that—spiritually poor. He is referring to those who, simply in terms of their own spiritual resources feel inadequate and broken and afraid.

Jesus presents us with a spiritually rich person in the figure of the Pharisee. Of such a person Jesus could only call them whitewashed tombs (Matthew 23:27). "Woe to you, you blind guides and Pharisees," he declares. "You say, if anyone swears by the altar, it is nothing, but if anyone swears by the gift that is on the altar, he is bound by the oath" (Matthew 23:16, 18, RSV). Here Jesus is pointing to one feature of the rich man: he takes his own gifts most seriously. And Jesus remarks, "You blind men! For which is greater, the gift or the altar which makes the gift sacred?" (Matthew 23:19, RSV). Here [again] Jesus is pointing to one of the features of rich men; they take their own gifts as good things. They do not realize how weak and silly from God's point of view are their offerings of knowledge and piety and property. They think God is lucky to have their allegiance, and so they swear by their gifts, rather than by the action of God at the altar by which God himself makes their gifts worthy of him.

And to these men Jesus concludes: "Woe to you, you scribes and Pharisees. You clean the outside of the cup and plate, but inside you are full of extortion and rapacity. First clean the inside of the cup, and then the outside also may be clean" (Matthew 23:25–26, RSV, with considerable alteration).

---

[3] The clauses in verse 4 are reversed in McGill's quotation, and RSV's "this child" becomes "the child."

Clean the inside. But how is a cup clean? By being emptied of all supposedly good things that are in it.

Any person who is not willing to be emptied, to let go of his own piety and his own faith and his own loving and his own virtue, he is full of extortion and rapacity, full of spiritual pride and greed.

Before the cross of Jesus, no one can claim to be an adequate lover, no one can pretend to be wise, no one can flaunt his own powerfulness. Wealth becomes impossible there, even at the deepest spiritual level.

But all this teaching of poverty by Jesus is only a comment on the poverty of his own actual experience, made unambiguously clear on the cross. The cross does not exhibit Jesus's virtue, or his knowledge, or his power. It kills him, and thus it exhibits his poverty.

III

This is an extremely difficult and an extremely offensive lesson. It seems silly and impractical. What of the problems and torments of poverty? How can the Christian be poor? What of his frustration? What of his fears? What of his shame before the judgment of others?

Because this seems all so preposterous and dangerous, it is easy to ignore this and pretend that Jesus said and was no such thing. It is easy to tell ourselves, Jesus wasn't against wealth. Not at all. He only demanded that the rich man be grateful for and unselfish with his possessions. Whatever you have, you should thank God for it, and you should use it to help others. But, we say to ourselves, provided we maintain these qualities, Jesus never questioned our right to have our wealth.

But to do this, we must avoid the real Jesus who dies on the cross. In his place we put Santa Claus, fat with contentment, rich with possessions for everyone, a perfect symbol for self-indulgence, that annual savior for our economy who speaks in the parables of the dollar sign and says, suffer the little children to come unto me [see Matthew 19:14, Mark 10:14, Luke 18:16].

This gospel of contentment with wealth must ignore Jesus, especially Jesus on the cross. For the child of God, as described by the New Testament and as presented in the person of Jesus, is only poor. In some peculiar way he may be strong and contented and even joyful in his poverty, but he is poor. And that is why the New Testament and Jesus are really concerned, not with rich people giving to the poor, but with rich people becoming poor. In other words, what Jesus calls for is not for us to be unselfish, but for us to be empty, to be needy, to be, in ourselves, impoverished.

IV

But clearly something is missing. How is it psychologically possible to want to be poor? There must be some new way of looking at poverty, some new factor in the situation that sets everything in a new light. Exactly. And the new factor is love. God's power, God's virtue, God's loving, in short God's love means wealth *as sufficient for us*.

The new factor is that God does not save us from evil by giving us possessions—material or spiritual possessions. He saves us from all evil by letting us live by and enjoy himself, the power he is in himself, the righteousness he is in himself.

Let us see more clearly: the righteousness of love before Jesus gives us only a sense of inadequacy and failure. If you want to feel good about your virtue, don't look at Jesus. Could you resist temptation? Could you forgive under torture?

Perhaps being a Christian means to have superior power? Note Paul [in] 2 Corinthians 4 ["But we have this treasure in earthen vessels, to show that the transcendent power belongs to God and not to us" (4:7)]. Before the cross of Christ, all pretense of power is called a lie. Who has power? Jewish priests, Roman [?] Sadducee, Pilate. What of the disciples?

Perhaps being a Christian means to have superior knowledge, knowledge of God, knowledge of human evil. Note Paul in our lesson. Before the cross of Jesus, no one is wise.

The child of God, the one who belongs to Christ is poor—materially and spiritually. No other message can be derived from the New Testament.

Why isn't this suicidal and impossible for us as persons? What of the evils of poverty: helplessness, frustration and shame? We cannot pretend that they are not there.

V

Now we come to the heart of the matter. The answer is the love of God. Love is the name for the frame of mind, for the attitude which does not mind being poor.

What is love? To want the other's good (love without selfishness). To affirm the other's good (love without envy). To live by the other's good (love without pride). This is the essence of the Christian life. A lover does not think about possession, does not want possession. That's about himself, but as a lover his thoughts are filled with the other.

This is love. Therefore selfishness and envy are not as important as pride. Giving of your wealth, which removes your selfishness, is less important than being poor,[4] which removes your pride. Pride is the real enemy of love.

The Christian state is like that of a child. The child does not receive from the father so the things become *his*. They remain the father's. Therefore there is no possession in giving [?] (Exodus 16).[5] Our spiritual goal is, therefore, God himself.

---

[4] See Sermon 6, p. 62.

[5] What a consequential word to be unsure of. Perhaps one wants the word to be "getting" or "receiving." But the pencil marks will not allow either. To say there is no possession in giving is true by definition. What if the force of the line is not descriptive but prescriptive? Is Exodus 16 a clue? No verse or verses are specified. This is the narrative of the hungry Israelites in the wilderness of Sin following the Exodus. The Lord, with characteristic concern about food, hears the "murmurings" of the people: "And the Lord said to Moses, 'I have heard the murmurings of the people of Israel; say to them, "At twilight you shall eat flesh, and in the morning you shall be filled with bread; then you shall know that I am the Lord your God"'" (Exodus 16:11–12). The bread is manna, but it will not keep—except when a two-day supply is given so that the sabbath might be respected. Is McGill's thought that the Lord gives (". . . I will rain bread from heaven for you; and the people shall go out and gather a day's portion every day . . ." [16:4], "When the Lord gives you in the evening flesh to eat and in the morning bread to the full . . ." [16:8], "And Moses said . . . 'It is the bread which the Lord has given you to eat . . .'" [16:15], "And Moses said . . . 'Let no man leave any of it till the morning . . .' But they did not listen to Moses; some left part of it till the morning, and it bred worms and became foul . . ." [16:19-20]) and *we receive*—but we must not seek to keep, hoard, possess? The dialectic of receiving and giving is vital—literally—for McGill. "Therefore there is no possession in giving" could characterize *the possibility of the recipient of receiving*. Receiving need not result in possession but in the dynamic push off of bestowal, of giving.

Jonah and Human Grandeur

Sermon delivered at First Parish Unitarian-Universalist
Church, Chelmsford, Massachusetts
February 20, 1977

*Now the word of the Lord came to Jonah the son of Amittai, saying, "Arise,
go to Nineveh, that great city, and cry against it; for their wickedness has
come up before me." But Jonah rose to flee to Tarshish from the presence
of the Lord. He went down to Joppa and found a ship going to Tarshish;
so he paid the fare, and went on board, to go with them to Tarshish, away
from the presence of the Lord.*

*But the Lord hurled a great wind upon the sea, and there was a mighty
tempest on the sea, so that the ship threatened to break up. Then the
mariners were afraid, and each cried to his god; and they threw the
wares that were in the ship into the sea, to lighten it for them. But Jonah
had gone down into the inner part of the ship and had lain down, and
was fast asleep. So the captain came and said to him, "What do you
mean, you sleeper? Arise, call upon your god! Perhaps the god will give a
thought to us, that we do not perish."*

*And they said to one another, "Come, let us cast lots, that we may know
on whose account this evil has come upon us." So they cast lots, and
the lot fell upon Jonah. Then they said to him, "Tell us, on whose account
this evil has come upon us? What is your occupation? And whence do
you come? What is your country? And of what people are you?" And he
said to them, "I am a Hebrew; and I fear the Lord, the God of heaven, who
made the sea and the dry land." Then the men were exceedingly afraid,
and said to him, "What is this that you have done!" For the men knew
that he was fleeing from the presence of the Lord,
because he had told them.*

Then they said to him, "What shall we do to you, that the sea may quiet down for us?" For the sea grew more and more tempestuous. He said to them, "Take me up and throw me into the sea; then the sea will quiet down for you; for I know it is because of me that this great tempest has come upon you." Nevertheless the men rowed hard to bring the ship back to land, but they could not, for the sea grew more and more tempestuous against them. Therefore they cried to the Lord, "We beseech thee, O Lord, let us not perish for this man's life, and lay not on us innocent blood; for thou, O Lord, hast done as it pleased thee." So they took up Jonah and threw him into the sea; and the sea ceased from its raging. Then the men feared the Lord exceedingly, and they offered a sacrifice to the Lord and made vows.

And the Lord appointed a great fish to swallow up Jonah; and Jonah was in the belly of the fish three days and three nights." (Jonah 1:1–17)

The story of Jonah is so familiar and so preposterous—three days in the belly of a whale—that we do not listen to it. For in this story—and it is a story—there appears perhaps the most crucial theme in the Old Testament.

The theme is the danger and the evil of grandeur and greatness, of any grandeur and greatness except the grandeur and greatness of God. Because God is just—is justice itself—God's grandeur is not a source of injustice. But this is not so with humans. When humans become preoccupied with their own grandeur, then they become unjust.

Because God is loving—is the very fullness of love—God's grandeur does not cut God off from love and make God hateful. But in humanity, when there is a preoccupation with grandeur, with achievement, with success, then love begins to die.

The theme of the danger and the evil of human greatness appears everywhere in the Old Testament. But it stands out in the story of Jonah.

The story opens with God's call to Jonah. "Go to the great city of Nineveh and denounce it for its wickedness." But Jonah fled to escape from the Lord and boarded a ship for Tarshish. Tarshish is believed to be a large coastal city in Spain, not far from the Straits of Gibraltar. In other words, Jonah wanted to get as far away from Nineveh as possible.

For us today Nineveh is only a dim name. It is hard for us to catch what is at stake in God's call to Jonah. In fact, by 300 B.C. Nineveh had vanished. No trace of it was left. Then in 1820 a British political agent stationed in Baghdad did some digging at two large mounds and discovered some ruins. Excavations were begun and continued for ninety years, until the remains of the whole huge ancient city of Nineveh were finally exposed.

Nineveh was one of the greatest cities in the Middle East from about 1300 B.C. when it became a royal city until its destruction seven hundred years later in 600 B.C. when it was sacked and totally destroyed by a combined assault of the Medes and the Babylonians.

In the last two hundred years of its existence it became one of the wonders of the ancient world, filled with palaces and lavish adornments. Several palaces were built with colored stones on the outside and cedar-wood on the inside. When later in the story of Jonah Jonah finally arrived at Nineveh, it had already reached its greatest magnificence. In Chapter 3 it reads: "Nineveh was a vast city, a three days' journey across" [Jonah 3:3].

When the story begins, no account is given of what exactly was going on in Nineveh, what its wickedness exactly was. But today we know that it secured its wealth from one of the most prolonged and systematic policies of exploitation and enslavement of that period. For instance, in the reigns of Sennacherib and Esarhaddon every people that these rulers conquered were forced to bring slaves and materials to adorn Nineveh. Its oppression and exploitation were extreme.

When we begin reading the book of Jonah, and when we hear simply of "the great city of Nineveh" and "its wickedness" [Jonah 1:2], with no further elaboration, nothing much registers with us.

But to those who belonged to the religion of the Old Testament, the point was obvious. The wickedness of Nineveh was expressed in its cruelty to the weak and the poor. But the origin of this particular wickedness and the center of its wickedness lay in its greatness. It was a great city, i.e. it was a human community devoted to making itself great, gathering itself into grandeur through wealth and technology and architecture and military power.

For us, of course, that must always seem to be a puzzling theme in the Old Testament. What is wrong with human grandeur? Why shouldn't a community try to magnify itself as much as possible? That is a very difficult and awkward theme for us who live in the United States because we belong to a community that is committed to its own grandeur. We should try to have the highest standard of living on earth, the strongest military might on earth, the most creative science on earth, the tallest buildings, the fastest roads, the best symphony orchestras, the most splendid hamburgers. In fact, every day of our lives we read advertisements which seduce us to go buy. Buy this product or that product, and other people will admire you.

Young people in our society are often brought up to succeed. What does it mean, "to succeed"? No child is taught that when he or she makes a specified amount of money a year—20,000 or 200,000 dollars—then he or she succeeds. No child is taught that to reach a certain specific level of skill in some work or trade or profession, then that is success. Not at all. For the urge to success is not the striving for some definite goal. The urge for success is nothing but the urge for grandeur, and there are no clear, definite limits for grandeur. The success that young people in our society are taught is not defined as the attainment of any specific goal. It is rather the striving for ever-increasing grandeur, ever-increasing wealth or beauty or skill or speed or whatever it is. And this impulse to grandeur by individuals is socially rewarded—with being given a Nobel Prize at the extreme and being included in the *Guinness Book of World Records* at the other extreme. The person who discovers the precise chemical process by which a cell in the human body becomes cancerous is very different from the person who holds his or her breath longer than anyone else in the world. But for all their different ambitions, both of these people are alike in that they strive for success, that is, they are committed to the quest for grandeur.

Therefore, since we in the United States teach each other that grandeur is the greatest thing in life, we might very well find it difficult and even annoying to come upon this Old Testament theme that exactly this hunger for human grandeur is the essence of human wickedness. What lies behind such a notion?

The reason is the problem of oppression. Oppression is not a series of particular actions. Oppression occurs when life is so arranged that some people constantly are exploited and deprived of the minimal necessities of life, including the need for dignity.

There may be occasions when one group of people oppress another out of fear, because those second people have a capacity to defeat the first. But that does not explain long, systematic oppression. That does not explain the neglect of the poor, the enslavement of the helpless. Fear is not causing this kind of oppression.

In the Old Testament the theme is proclaimed by the historians and the prophets and the Psalmists that this oppression—this prolonged systematic crushing of the weak and helpless—arises in people who are committed to human grandeur. In other words, oppressors are the people who are determined to succeed.

The reason for this is obvious. When you want to succeed, when you want to raise human existence to a higher and fuller level, to a new grandeur, then it is that weakness and poverty, sickness and failure are so intolerable psychologically. When failure occurs elsewhere, we scorn. For instance, when we hear how the farmers of India plough with oxen we scorn their primitiveness and relish the grandeur of our great farm machines that can do the job in one-hundredth of the time. But when failure occurs among those who are supposed to be great, then we become furious.

Here we are in the United States trying to be the greatest nation in the world, and New York City is going bankrupt. That is outrageous! Here I am wanting my child to succeed, and at the piano recital he goofs up the playing of his piece of music. Outrageous!

You see, the desire for grandeur is exactly what makes us intolerant of human weakness and failure. The fact that perhaps everyone of us in this room has been brought up to be ashamed of failure, to fear and flee from failure—this shows how deeply the desire for grandeur has worked into our inner lives. And if we are intolerant of our own failures, no amount of liberal toleration and good will ever quite cover over our deep contempt for those others who fail, those who do not contribute to the search for grandeur. Whether we decide to let the failures suffer and pay for their failures, or decide to take care of the failures with charity, there is a basic contempt for them in both cases. In both cases, those who fail are thought to have lost their dignity.

In the way I have been speaking, it would seem that the reason why human grandeur is wrong is that it leads to injustice. Indeed, it does. But that is not the only reason it is wrong.

It is also wrong, not because of the things it produces like contempt and oppression. It is wrong in itself. For in the perspective of the Old Testament grandeur and glory belong properly only to God. God holds the foundations of the earth in God's hands. All the heavens and the earth declare God's majesty. When we are aware of the glory of God, then all human striving for glory becomes pathetic. By comparison with God's inconceivable glory, the greatest civilization in the history of the world is just as insignificant as the earliest Paleolithic community of people whose only tools were shaped stones. When we set the modern Americans in comparison with such people from the stone-age, the Americans indeed seem to attain a grandeur. But when we measure the Americans by the glory of God, then the Americans seem as nothing.

And, of course, when we are freed from having to make ourselves into vessels of grandeur, when we are freed from the compulsion to succeed, then we can accept our failures just as readily as our success. Then we can grant dignity as much to those who fail as to those who succeed. Then we can accept the frailties and the limitations of our human way.

In the story of Jonah, we hear that Jonah was swallowed by a whale and lived three days in its belly. But people who live in the dream of grandeur are also, as it were, in the belly of a monster. This desire for grandeur envelops them and cuts them off from their human life. Many people have been swallowed alive by the monster of human grandeur, and live in the belly of that monster, not three days as Jonah did, but for their entire lives.

We can now understand the words of the prophet Micah, which President Carter quoted in his inauguration address.[1] "What does the Lord require of you? To do justly, to love mercy and to walk humbly with your God" [Micah 6:8]. The last is the key to the other two. When we know and affirm that glory belongs to God and not to us—and that is what it means to "Walk humbly with your God"—when we give up all striving for human grandeur in our society and in ourselves, only then we can "do justly" to the failures and weaknesses in our neighbors. Only then can we "love mercy" for our own failures and weaknesses.

In short, humanism—real authentic humanism—begins when the human craving for grandeur is removed. And that is the issue involved in God's call to Jonah: "Go to the great city of Nineveh and denounce it for its wickedness." God was not sending Jonah in order to improve Nineveh, in order to make Nineveh better and more pleased with itself. God was not sending Jonah to help Nineveh fulfill its desire for its own grandeur.

On the contrary, Jonah was to go and remind Nineveh of the glory of the Lord Almighty, so that Nineveh might be delivered from its hypnotic and destructive preoccupation with its own grandeur so that Nineveh might realize that the human may be only human—only relatively good and only successful in modest ways now and then—so that Nineveh might come down from its magnificence and be more human to the weak and the poor.

We must remember this: the wickedness of Nineveh—alas!—is the wickedness of the United States, and the oppressiveness of Nineveh appears also in the United States. And the danger is deep upon us that anyone who fails—the sick, the aged, the insane, the criminals—any who mar our American hunger for grandeur are thereby simply worthless and must be thrown away like trash.

> O Lord,[2]
> the winter days are upon us and within us.
> We too are as cold as the earth.
> The fires by which we seek to warm ourselves do not
>   always reach very deeply into us.
> O God, give us a warmth and a fire into our deepest
>   centers.

[1] 20 January 1977.

[2] Interestingly, at least as the manuscript indicates, McGill moves into this prayer with no indication, no "Let us pray." How would one ever find the reference for this extended prayer? No need: the prayer is unmistakably McGill. The prayer is dialectically remarkable, moving without warning from McGillian-perceived wrongheadedness to McGillian-intended genuine prayer. The form of the prayer represents the form of McGill's manuscript (to the extent that this is possible).

We would thank you, O Father, for your care during this
   past week.
Some have died, but the fabric of our lives has not been
   strained.
Neither war nor famine nor epidemic nor economic chaos
   has touched us.
For this, O God, we would thank you—except we do not
   feel this very much. So it's been another good week.
   What else is new? The benefits to our lives are so
   ample, so extensive that sometimes we can only yawn.
We see nightmare elsewhere—the starvation in Africa, the
   social turmoil in Northern Burma. But we turn from
   these distresses.

Your goodness, O Lord, has made our hearts fat, and we
   are too contented and too complacent to be able to
   feel much gratitude.
Forgive our inadequacy, the coldness of our hearts and
   bring them warmth.

Yet also, O God our Father, we are living in ordeals.
The school, the marriage, the job, a sickness in the body,
   an anxiety or a depression in the spirit—we carry
   these. We hide from them, and yet we carry them.
Teach us your forgiveness through our forgiving one
   another. Teach us not to reject and condemn what
   is weak in ourselves and what is offensive in our
   loved ones. Teach us to accept ourselves in all our
   limitations, as you accept us and love us, in and with
   our coldness and failure.

O Lord, turn us outward toward our neighbors.
As we learn to accept weakness in ourselves, let us also
   learn to accept and nourish the weaknesses that we
   see in others. Before the suffering, the loneliness, the
   destitution of another, help us not be cold in our
   response.
And as we learn to praise you for the strength that is in
   ourselves, let us also learn to praise the goodness in
   others, without envy or resentment.

Give us cleaner hearts, O Lord, give us cleaner hearts.

We would pray for all our governing officials, that they
    may be sheltered from personal despair and may
    continue to defend our lives from every chaos. We
    would pray for those who are delegated to protect our
    lives—the judge, the police, military people, doctors,
    nurses, paramedics, teachers, lawyers, parents.
For their care help us to be grateful and not angry. For the
    inadequacies help us to be merciful and not vengeful.

Let humility not be shame, but a restoring of peace with
    ourselves in your care.
Let us practice tolerance with our own needs and our own
    failures and our own deformities, for only then can we
    nourish the hungry and support their failures without
    feeling fear and scorn.
O Lord, deliver us from our urge for grandeur and from all
    the demonic oppressions of ourselves and of each other
    which that urge brings.
O God, give us this peace, for this is the peace which
    passes all understanding.

In the week ahead, O God, lift up our hearts that we may
    praise you. Lift up our eyes that we may see our needy
    neighbors. Lift up our minds that, in the knowledge of
    your Lordship over all of life, we may face the tragedies
    of our existence without terror or blame.

Now, O Lord, each of us in the silence of our hearts will
    pray in gratitude for our own joys, in grief for our own
    sins, and in beseeching for our own needs.

Suffering

Sermon delivered at Harvard Divinity School

So much misery. It is God's failure—this is a great theme in our century. There is a longing for a direct move away from miseries and outrage and helplessness and savagery to peace and strength. We cry out to God and there is no answer.[1] We are longing for a movement into a peace without conflict.

Yet from the beginning—in response especially to Jesus's crucifixion— there has been in the churches another way, another expectation.

Blessed are the poor, sorrowful, those who are hungry and thirsty [see Matthew 5:3–4, 6]. Do we forgive in order to effect a change in others, so that when that change fails and others remain obdurate we may cease forgiving? Forgive seventy times seven times [see Matthew 18:22], without [?] on success.

Always the life of sharing insisted on by Jesus does not serve immediately and directly to bring forth the good life. God's rule is not identified with the removal of the negatives from life. The cross of Christ is not a display of what we are expecting from Christ to avoid. On the contrary as Jesus advises in a saying in Matthew, "Pupils should be content to share their teachers lot, and the servants to share the lot of their masters" [Matthew 10:25, after NEB].

The life of sharing involves receiving and giving, involves being open and vulnerable. The great danger is to convert the problem of suffering into a problem of the capacity for suffering in ourselves. Then we dread, not suffering, but rather that neediness and that vulnerability which makes us susceptible

---

[1] A reminder of editorial decision: McGill often writes in notes. His manuscript for the opening of this sermon is as follows: "So much misery. God's failure—great theme in our century. longing for a direct move away from miseries and outrage and helplessness and savagery to peace and strength. Cry out to God and no answer." Etc. Rather than burden the text with brackets with each addition of an article or pronoun, brackets have been omitted. Brackets are employed when more distinctive additions are made.

to suffering. The dangerous hope is this: O Lord, make us so we cannot weep, cannot pain, cannot need. Make us invulnerable.

If the meaning of life were the removal of miseries, the elimination of all agonies and guilt, then the gift of invulnerability would indeed be the essential, the decisive mark of God's goodness. Then we would be essentially free, totally free—not just from the actual miseries—but from their very possibility.

Yet if there were that gift of invulnerability, that ability to escape need, then, while we should be free from the ordeal of suffering and oppression, we should also be free from that sharing which is the kernel of the life of Christ. To share with one another, to share with Christ, to share with God, there must be receiving and not simply giving. There must be need for the other. There must be vulnerability, that is, the being open in our common and individual existence to the entrance of others. To grow in the life from Christ, we must perfect those very conditions in ourselves which make us subject to suffering—our neediness by which we may receive from God and from each other, and yet by which others may starve and empty us, or by which we may starve and empty others—and our vulnerability by which our central beings are open to God and to one another, and yet by which others may violate and oppress us, and we may violate and oppress others.

In the New Testament traditions, the rich are held up as the ones who establish themselves against evil by becoming free from need. In that invulnerability, "How hard it is for the wealthy to enter the kingdom of heaven" (Mark 10:23 [see Matthew 19:23, Luke 18:24]).

Suffering as such is never good, never fruitful, never the purpose of God. The good never comes from suffering as such, as if we must suffer for a period before we are allowed to move out of suffering.

But the movement toward the fostering of those conditions which make us capable of suffering, and which make suffering possible—this movement constitutes a horizon where not suffering, but isolation, hard-heartedness, and invulnerability are the ultimate abomination.

The joy of Jesus is not primarily a direct flight from grief; the peace of Jesus is not a direct escape from conflict. And the forgiveness of Jesus does not effect a direct removal of pernicious action. This joy and peace and forgiveness belong to mutual sharing.

The primary work of the Church is not simply to remove suffering as such, but rather to nourish a fellowship where vulnerability is treasured and needs are authorized and met.

But the temptations to escape neediness and to secure invulnerability are often forceful. It is subtle temptation always to become hypnotized by the enormity of evil and to long primarily for its removal.

The focus of God's claim in Jesus is rather for the growth and rootage of human existence in that receiving which is based on neediness, and in that sharing which opens boundaries and involves vulnerability.

Yet no instance of the temptation to refuse these qualities is more destructive than the effort to worship an unneedy and invulnerable God. If such a God indeed excludes every possibility of needy brokenness, this God also excludes the life actualized in Jesus. For this God is not the creator of shared life but simply a product of the human outrage at evil. This God canonizes the life of wealth.

If God's rule in Jesus Christ points away from suffering, it is not because God stands in inviolable self-sufficiency. Such self-containedness is precisely a source of human suffering, the avarice and arrogance to exclude neediness from ourselves, and the heartless refusal to respond to the neediness in others.

The love of God sanctifies our neediness for God and for one another, because neediness belongs properly and naturally to God.

Needed
—An Education in Poverty[1]

Baccalaureate Address delivered at Harvard, ca. 1974

*Greater love has no man than this, that a man
lay down his life for his friends. (John 15:13)*

In our society, at the end of every phase of schooling there is what we call a "commencement," a celebration of beginnings. The reason is obvious enough: schooling is only preparation and prelude. It exists only to lead on to what lies ahead. For those who will receive degrees tomorrow, this is a commencement, because the future for which they have been preparing is about to become actual.

Nothing makes clearer why this is a moment of deep disquiet and anxiety. For all the conflicts and frustrations which beset our life in the United States today make it difficult to face the future with assured enthusiasm. American life is in the midst of some deep and obscure torment.

At the level of circumstance there are extraordinary problems in every area—the senseless burden of the Vietnam War, the suffering of the deprived minorities, the violence of police and national guard, the power of organized crime, the deep confusions about drugs, about sexual behavior, and the massive control by the Pentagon of American money, American resources and American manpower.

But the torment is not simply in terms of these circumstances, however compelling they may be. Their accumulative effect is to raise a question about deep values and directions.

The anguish reaches to the center of the impulses that shape and guide American life. All commencements today—from births in the maternity

---

[1] An alternative title, scratched out and following the title above: "Wealth—the Great Deception."

wards to new national policies and leaders—bring these deep anxieties into focus. It is this level of anxiety which I will consider with you this evening. And I will try to answer this question: exactly what kind of confidence is being threatened and gutted by today's events? What have American people counted on—all people, young and old, men and women, black and white, the educational elite and the dispossessed minorities—what assurance have they had that is now beginning to turn to ashes and the failure of which is driving them to uncertainty, to fear, to anger, and occasionally to violence?

I

Because of their neediness, human beings have always been victimized. They have been victimized by other individuals, institutions or by nature and circumstances beyond human control, by what are legally known as "acts of God." A child is born mentally retarded; a young woman is disfigured by fire; a nation of millions suffers prolonged drought with devastating famine.

One typical response is for people to try to acquire something—some knowledge, or some resource—that will protect them from this deprivation. They may develop plastic surgery for burned faces, or a water-storage and irrigation system for drought. They try to defend themselves against the slings and arrows of fortune[2] by securing something in their control, or in their possession, or in their being which will save and restore them in the face of every danger.

I call this response to disaster the technique of having, since it is by having available some object or skill or resource that people may cope with a threatening evil. For most societies such having is no more than an impossible hope or a matter of unexpected good fortune. But in the United States this successful having is often taken as a fact.

You know the expression: "We are the richest nation in the world. How can we have poverty?" Consider this statement carefully. It states two facts, first that the United States is the richest nation in the world, and secondly, that there is poverty here. But notice how it interprets these two facts. By its tone and style, this statement gives the impression that in a country like the United States poverty should not exist. It thus attaches a very different importance to these two facts. It expresses surprise that there is poverty. The second fact is taken as unexpected. In other words, it looks upon richness and wealth as the true, the basic, the essential and controlling condition of life in the United States. It reflects the belief that American initiative, or American know-how, or American technology or American unselfishness is such that we in this country really can remove all poverty, all misery and suffering.

[2] See William Shakespeare, *Hamlet*, III, i.

If not actually removed, these evils have become in a sense accidental. They no longer belong to the inner and inescapable fabric of life. If they occur it is because something went wrong, some fluke happened, the normal adequacy of our skills and resources somehow momentarily failed. Normally and properly, life in the United States is a matter of everyone's having enough to satisfy him and protect him. Poverty and inadequacy are abnormal conditions. We are the richest nation in the world. How can we have poverty?

Once we identify this attitude, it is easy to see it running deeply through the whole fabric of American life. Listen to how Americans greet each other. At a party close your eyes and concentrate carefully on the tones in their voices. "How are you?" "Fine! Fine! Fine!" The questions and answers are always optimistic, always affirmative. They are in fact preliminary social reminders that we are permitted to deal with one another only in terms of an assurance that we have it made, and that our sufferings and inadequacies are no more than passing accidents.

Look at the advertisements, which present to us a colorful world of healthy, happy people, a world where something is available for every kind of trouble—drugs for pain, distraction for boredom, vacations for exhaustion, and credit cards for unrealized dreams. A clothing store recently described this American sense of things. I quote:

> A look of confidence comes with today's "New breed of man." He is satisfied with his achievements. He knows his deficiencies and he does something about them, dealing with such challenges as they appear. This is an "all-man" man. There may be others who recognize their deficiencies and merely accept them as fate, with a philosophical shrug of the shoulders. They must admire others. Don't be defeatist. Chances are that SHE (all capitals, of course) [McGill's parentheses] likes to think of you as an all-man man—a man with confidence. Right?[3]

Close quote. Right!

If this attitude seems rather fatuous here, there is nothing fatuous about its control of our entire educational effort. There one single philosophy tends to dominate over all others, the belief that each person should become all that he was created capable of being, that he should realize his full capacities, should expand to his full growth, and should show himself finally in his own shape and stature. Education functions to help each American to develop the

---

[3] Sampson's of 5th Avenue, *New York Sunday Times Magazine* [? 1974] 107. Page but no date! Well, we can live without this reference. The *Sunday Times* was unhelpful. My research says that Sampson's is out of business—because of that advertisement?

wealth within his own personal self, and thus to help him make his own rich contribution to our common life.

Courtship and marriage are usually conceived in the same way. As the phrase goes, it is a matter of "attracting" someone, which means, of having such personal richness and of so displaying it that someone of the other sex will respond. Courtship, like everything else, thus becomes a matter of securing available wealth.

Look at the moral development of American children. No child is taught: you will constantly find yourself with needs that cannot be satisfied, with fears that cannot be appeased, with destructive circumstances that cannot be controlled; therefore, learn courage and endurance, learn not to be emotionally overthrown by unrelieved pain and unforeseen disaster. Not a moment is wasted teaching such negative virtues to American children. On the contrary, need and poverty are only abnormal accidents. No one prepares for them; everyone prepares to avoid them. American children are morally developed with those virtues that help them acquire some kind of richness. If they have ambition, self-confidence, a willingness to work, a tolerance of routine and capacity for putting off their immediate satisfactions and devote themselves to long range goals, then they will get ahead. They will have the resources necessary to handle all their needs and disasters.

Finally, look at the kind of Christianity which has prevailed in the United States. What do American Christians usually believe? Two things. First, they believe that God is good and loving because he created for us a land and a way of life rich enough to nourish and satisfy us. Secondly, they believe that the primary duty for men is to make full use of these riches, but to do so unselfishly, to share what each has with the poor and underprivileged. As God's goodness consists in bestowing riches on us, so we should bestow our riches on one another. Following these lines, American Christians place the climax of their whole religious life at Christmas-time, when they can indulge in a bacchanalia of expensive giving and receiving.

In the United States wealth is not just a fact. It is a state of mind; it is a central and tap-root value. At point after point in our daily lives, we show how convinced we are that we have solved the problems of human existence by the technique of having. By encouraging individual freedom, by giving a talent-oriented education, by seeking out the natural resources in every continent, by exploiting those resources with the full productive power of technology, and by training people not to accept their deficiencies but to secure a variety of riches for every need. The American way of life has been marked by extraordinary confidence. Therefore we should really speak here, not of a technique of having, but of a gospel of having. Gospel meaning good news, and for much of America, wealth is the good news, that which will save us and redeem us from all evil. The wealth of money, the wealth of scientific knowledge, the wealth of social diversity, the wealth of individual opportunity, the wealth of military power, the wealth of international prestige, the wealth of God's unreserved goodness to us—America the beautiful, toward which all history moves.

II

As I read things today, this is the confidence which is now being undermined. Because of circumstances, people are less and less certain that American wealth is adequate to cope with the needs and sufferings, with the responsibilities and injustices in which the American people are involved. It is not a question of whether some other nation might be richer. Not at all. It is the unnerving thought that no amount of riches will be enough, that no amount of American fair-play will overcome the subtle and systematic oppression of black people, that no amount of welfare will ever redeem the areas of hardcore poverty, that no amount of expert intelligence or moral dedication will get us out of Vietnam with honor or out of pollution with safety, and that no amount of quiet humane reason will socialize our rioting youth, with their long hair, their refusal to work or to fight for this country. Every social disturbance, every legalized or illegialized murder, every economic uncertainty, and every confusion at the level of national policy brings anxiety. Every crisis concerns a particular situation and particular people whose violence or suffering or incompetence assaults us in the news report. But in addition, all these incidents keep eating away at our basic confidence, keep alive the question of whether the manifold richness of America is really any basis for the full life. Perhaps it is just a facade, that succeeds only by covering up people's suffering and poverty and desolation but not by saving them from these evils.

In fact, it does not take much living to realize that this gospel of having does not work. Who can measure the terrible inner boredom and sense of meaningless which the housewife endures in her mechanical kitchen? The young man strains for some achievement, some skill but when he attains it he finds that it is used by institutions he hardly understands, for purposes of profit and power that he cannot fully accept. Do you imagine that when parents have a child taken from them—killed by an irresponsible automobile driver, or destroyed by a war that seems senseless, or sent to prison for possession of drugs, or driven to aimless wandering by a despair that has no voice—do you imagine that they have riches to nourish them in this devastation? Can one measure the burdens of silent alienation which must be borne between some parents and children, and between some husbands and wives? Ravages are everywhere, from the Vietnam battlefield to the marriage bedroom. Take any swinger, take any all-man man with the kind of outer confidence described in the advertisement I read, who strides with assurance and seems to have everything under control—just scratch his surface and we will find so much self-distrust, so much poverty of values and goals, so much secret suffering.[4]

Perhaps the most compelling challenge to the gospel of having is posed by the aged. As people grow old, it becomes more and more unnatural for them to sustain their lives and their sense of being human by having riches. To grow old means to enter a stage of life where possessions and skills are only burdens, a stage where poverty becomes wholly natural.

People of course can go on for quite a while with an affirmative style, but in the end [time?] gets them, or disgust or age or lack of proper diet or boredom or children in college, or a broken leg while skiing in Switzerland, or a promotion, or new politics or new wives or just natural change and decay.

We remember these people when they were younger, when they exuded the gospel of wealth, when they looked for ten rounds on the golf course or laughed and drank for three days at the ski resort, but now they are just something under a sheet, or a cross or a stone, or under an easy delusion, packing a Bible or a golf bag or a briefcase—how they go! How they go! All the ones you never thought would go.

These things have always been known. In the past, it has been easy to imagine that all this suffering was a private disaster, characterizing individuals here and there, unfortunate points where the wealth of our American way of life did [not] quite come in time. Today, however, public events force the deeper question. Perhaps these instances of suffering are not exceptions and accidents. Perhaps poverty and destitution belong as much to the central fabric of American life as to the lives of people in the most under-developed country. We look at our involvement with the world as a whole, and discover that the very power on which we counted has in fact enmeshed us in a war that kills our youth, and drains our economy, and divides our society. We look at our technology, and find it polluting our air and water with a momentum that will be difficult to stop.

If this is true, if riches do not really enrich life at its deep level, then this gospel of having, this confidence in wealth itself becomes a source of panic. For there is no distress like that of believing in something which you

---

[4] At this point, McGill quotes in full the poem by Langston Hughes, "Minstrel Man," in *The Collected Works of Langston Hughes*, vol. 1, *The Poems: 1921–1940,* ed. Arnold Rampersad (Columbia: University of Missouri Press, 2001) 171–72. Curiously, McGill's own reference is "('Minstrel Man,' Anon.)." The reader will find the full text at: http://www.americanpoems. com/poets/Langston-Hughes/2390.

secretly know may be false. For much of your psychic energy must now go into avoiding the signs which discredit your belief. It is no accident, then, that Americans cannot tolerate the presence of poverty. This is not really because of charity or brotherly love. It is terror—terror that the presence of poor people will discredit the gospel of wealth, will show the essential inadequacy of all our riches, will in fact compel us to develop the virtues of courage and patience and endurances, which the gospel of wealth has promised us we would never need.

You will find no beggars on the streets of the United States [!], no deformed humans claiming you with their deformity. You will not visit many homes where an aged person is present who must be spoon fed. We remove the sick and the disabled—all of us do—and we must, because we are trained to use all our energies for handling wealth, and because none of us dares to be one with the poor. Shaped by the gospel of wealth, we have no choice but to place the aged and the disabled in institutions, and to make those institutions so beautifully landscaped, with such well manicured lawns that when we drive by them we cannot imagine the suffering that goes on within their walls.

And when a pregnant woman today learns that the child growing within her may be—or will be—deformed, she may well have an abortion. This is not because she lacks love. It is much deeper than that. It is because she has been brought up on the rich man's gospel. With all of us, she believes that life in the true sense is only for the rich and the whole, and that a child who will be physically impoverished cannot truly live, and therefore should not be forced to endure an empty existence.

Against this background, as long as we believe in the gospel of wealth, how is it possible to acknowledge our inadequacies and destitutions? How can the President possibly leave Vietnam without some sense of victory and success? How can he let it be a mark of America's diplomatic failure or military incompetence and moral inadequacy?

Voices today, and perhaps voices in each of us, are not only asking the rich man's usual question: How shall I use my resources to solve this problem? Rather the voices are asking: Perhaps reliance on resources is not the way. Perhaps we have been deceived by America's apparent wealth, or have deceived ourselves. Perhaps we must learn to bear poverty, to endure suffering without panic or evasion. Perhaps we must learn how to be human while bearing pain and destitution, while bearing precisely those agonies which, according to the rich man's gospel, make humane life impossible.

III

In this situation, I would remind you that if Jesus Christ, in the New Testament, represents anything at all, he gives men a call to poverty. He does not identify God's goodness with worldly riches; he does not identify human fulfillment with the possession of worldly resources; and he does not identify human goodness with the sharing of worldly goods.

When he calls upon the rich young man to give all that he has to feed the poor, he does not mean: give your surplus time and your extra pint of blood and your unneeded wealth. He means clearly and unambiguously: give so as to enter the state of poverty yourself. When Jesus says, "There is no greater love than this, that a man lay down his life for his friends" [John 15:13], he does not mean lay down the unimportant aspects of your life, your merely physical existence. He means lay down the entire extent of your vitality. If the Christian Church has taken the cross as its symbol, an instrument of barbaric execution, this is in recognition of the fact that Jesus himself lived toward the most total destitution imaginable, the destitution of death, and never lived for the sake of having riches at his disposal.

We here confront a challenge to the gospel of wealth at a far more serious level. For in this aspect of Jesus's life, we are not being told simply that poverty is real and therefore we have to accept it. On the contrary, he calls men to poverty as the fullest and deepest and finest human condition. He declares that the gospel of wealth is not just untrue; he condemns it as evil and humanly bankrupt. Today we are also hearing voices which share this conviction, and which affirm that poverty is the most liberating, the most satisfying and the most richly authentic human condition, that poverty and not wealth is the true good news.

I know that rich people have always found this view perverse and incredible. They look upon Jesus's destitution on the cross as a nightmare, and never call that Friday Good Friday. For them, that Friday is the very opposite of everything good. Consider, however, two things.

First, as long as we live in terms of what we can possess, of riches that we can have available, our life becomes limited to the kinds of goods that we can control; that is, goods cut down to our human level. This is not a question of what kind of riches we seek. This simply points to the fact that any riches which have to come under our control must be small enough for us to manage.

But every human being knows that in life there are also goods utterly beyond human control, that the heart can know joys, not in terms of any riches it possesses, but in terms of powers and enormities utterly beyond its control, powers which on their own move in and transfigure our whole existence. We would think here of romantic love, where a person is caught up in a dazzle and glory that does not arise from anything he controls or owns, and that seems to take possession of him from utterly beyond his familiar experience. This is the condition of ecstasy.

Obviously, the state of ecstasy involves and requires poverty. It means letting go of our possessions and the identity which our talents and our riches give us. It means being willing to become a person enveloped and irradiated by a different order of splendor, by a power beyond possession. Anyone who has loved ecstatically knows that in that condition he or she lives in a state where riches have absolutely no meaning. When Jesus calls men to poverty, it is that they may be emptied of small and sterile goods, of the goods cut down to the proportions of human control, and thereby filled with a transcendent good, with the glory of God. In that sense, no one can ever be related to God by way of possession, but only by way of being possessed. The price of ecstasy is poverty. The gospel of wealth therefore gives only small joys and creates situations where the imagination dies and where ecstasy disappears in boredom. Since all the riches of this world may be a gift of the devil and [earthly kings?]—I should [have] thought I worshipped the devil if I thanked my God for worldly things.

There is a second thing to be remembered. Death awaits us and death is total destitution. No one possesses in the realm of death. You take absolutely nothing with you, not your knowledge or your personality or your virtue or your reputation. Therefore people who believe in the gospel of wealth, who identify the possibility of significant life with what they can possess—such people can only look upon death as the annihilation of life. This is not because they deliberately adopt this view of death. Not at all. This is because they understand the possibility of life as requiring available possessions. Death is the end of all possessions, and therefore for them it is the absolute zero, the unthinkable emptiness.

In the realm of Jesus, there are no possessions. Even faith is not something possessed, and in the garden of Gethsemane, before his arrest, under the pressure of immanent[5] death, even Jesus loses his possession of religious assurance. "My God, my God—why have you forsaken me?" [Matthew 27:46; Mark 15:34]. But for Jesus dispossession is not the loss of life, but the condition of life, of ecstatic identity. To live by what is utterly beyond our possession means that losing everything we have is not the end, but the beginning. That is why Jesus's call to poverty is also a call to death, to take up his cross into that final destitution.

---

[5] McGill indeed writes "immanent." Does he intend "imminent"? But "immanent" also accords with McGill's thinking.

IV

Let us now come back to today—to you who now graduate from one or another aspect of university work. Have I said anything that you yourselves do not already know?

You complete an education which has been designed to perfect your richness, in a specialized way at the graduate or professional schools, but in a broader way, involving social and athletic life, at the college. Nowhere have you been taught to come to terms with your inescapable neediness, with that poverty and self-distrust and inadequacy which underlie the poses of wealth you have been trained to carry.

It might be well to think of this time as a commencement in two ways. Now begins a new and more responsible exercise of the personal wealth which your education has given you. At the same time, now also begins a more serious and more inescapable wrestle with your essential poverty. Now begins in earnest your coming to terms with limitations, inadequacies and irreparable emptiness. Now begins the search for courage, for patience, above all, for humility, so that these negatives will not simply lacerate you and terrify you. Now begins your preparation for the vocation of dying.

You will have few teachers in the United States. You may possibly learn from your parents, but this is difficult. American parents confront their children with such a demand for richness that the sharing of negatives, of fixed failures and permanent despairs is almost unthinkable. You may well have to proceed alone. But do proceed. Grasp your poverty positively. And though for this you will receive no applause and perhaps only hostility, to those near you may become more valuable than all of your professors.

Recognize the connection between poverty and truth, between poverty and death, and between poverty and ecstasy, recall the words of Augustine, a Christian who lived 1600 years ago: "It is more blessed to be one of the poor than to serve the poor."[6]

---

[6] The quest for this quotation continues. McGill gives no reference. Meanwhile, I thank Father Thomas Martin, Ordo Sancti Augustini, Director, The Augustinian Institute, Villanova, Pennsylvania, for bringing us into the vicinity of this theme. See John E. Rotelle, ed., *The Works of Saint Augustine, Sermons I* (1–19) (Brooklyn: New City, 1990) 293–96 (sermon 11), *Sermons II* (20–50) (1990) 226–33, 344–52 (sermons 41 and 50), *Sermons III/4* (94A–147A [1992]) 164–69 (sermon 113). The closest text is: "So who are the least ones of Christ? They are those who have said goodbye to all their possessions and followed him, and have distributed whatever they had among the poor . . ." (sermon 113, 164).

II

Kinds of
Power, Death, and Love

*"This is the essential purpose
and value of pure speech:
it enables us not to be alone,
without the risk—or power—of self-expenditure
[the power of self-expenditure is also death and love]."*
—Sermon 10

Be Angry

I was dumb and silent,
I held my peace to no avail;
*   my distress grew worse,*
*   my heart become hot within me.*
As I mused, the fire burned;
*   then I spoke with my tongue:*
"Lord, let me know my end,
*   and what is the measure of my days;*
*   let me know how fleeting my life is!"*
(Psalm 39:2–4)

May words of our lips and meditations of our hearts be acceptable in your sight, O God of our salvation.

"You have learned that our forefathers were told, 'Do not commit murder. Anyone who commits murder must be brought to judgment.' But what I tell you is this: Anyone who nurses anger against his brother must be brought to judgment" (Matthew 5:21–22a, NEB). The command of Jesus that we should love and not hate one another has been interpreted in our day in a very definite way. It is taken to mean that all hate and anger should be avoided in our relations with others. In other words, the command of Jesus to love and not to hate is taken to be a rule for how we can manage our everyday lives. By his command Jesus is showing us how to run our daily existence in the pleasantest way.

Surely this is totally false. That is, whatever else Jesus may have been doing, he was not trying to help people find devices and technique to improve their daily lives. He was not trying to do this because he was concerned with God. And God, as the beginning and end of all things, cannot be degraded into some device for improving our everyday lives. Getting through each day as best we can is certainly a legitimate area of concern. It is the area of insurance policies and personal tact, of deodorants and money. But it is not the area where we meet and know the love of God. It is not the area within which Jesus calls us to discover the goodness of God. God simply does not serve us at that level—at the level of deodorants and insurance policies and personal tact. Jesus was crucified, and furthermore his crucifixion has always been seen in the Christian communities as a good—essential event for dealing with the deep agonies of human existence. That is why in the Christian churches we call the day of his death *Good* Friday—not bad Friday or dreadful Friday. But his death also means that whatever he may represent, he does not represent a successful technique for handling everyday life. On that score Jesus is obviously a total failure. He did not manage life very well. He did not help people to avoid violence and upheaval; he did [not][1] assist them to get through each day a little better—putting on the right manner here, adopting a little tact there, taking sensible precautions at another point. Jesus has nothing for us at that level of life, because that is simply not the level where the meaning of God or the goodness of God can ever be found. God is the last horizon. God is the ultimate beginning. God is final end, the end beyond all ends. God is at the deepest center of ourselves: God is at the ultimate reach of our spirits. When Jesus speaks and acts in God's name, he is addressing us at that deepest level and final horizon of our existence. Anyone who does not want to be addressed there, who only wants to live in terms of his or her everyday life—that person has lost God. For that person, Jesus in his authentic claims on us will make no sense at all, will seem either like a fool or a devil. Therefore, when Jesus commands love and not hate, he is speaking of our deep and fundamental attitudes. He is not speaking of the masks we wear and the techniques we use to get along with each other.

Let us ask about the situation we meet today: the situation when Jesus' command to love and not to hate is used to keep people from being angry at each other, is used to encourage them to adopt an agreeable and cooperative manner, at all times.

What lies behind their use of Jesus to foster the particular tactic of pleasantness in human relationships? The answer, I think, is this: we are a people who are genuinely frightened of all negative emotions, like anger or hate or envy.[2] These feelings distress us. They seem so destructive, so unmanageably

[1]   McGill writes "did assist"; but "not" is certainly intended.

[2]   There is something of a scratch out here for the next twelve lines: "When we hear Jesus calling us to love and not to hate, we usually think of 'to walk the second mile and to turn the other cheek' [see Matthew 5:41, 39], we usually think of this in a simple way. What attitude should I have? Should I let other people know that I am angry or should I at least try to maintain the appearance that I like them?

"But this is not the way it is with us human beings. Because we do not feel free to show either emotion–either hate or love–we are not free to choose love. We all belong to a community of people who are frightened of all the negative emotions, like anger and hate and envy."

destructive. And therefore we try to block them, to stifle them. We try to get our children to fear these emotions, so that they will suppress them. If they dislike someone, we ask them at least to be polite. If they are angry, we ask them to keep it inside, not to let it come through.[3]

When we look at our lives, it is really astonishing how little dignity we give to anger, how much we use Christianity to cover up this feeling and to help us pretend that this feeling is not there. We are supposed to be nice and positive toward other people.

I remember, several years ago, speaking in New York City on a panel with a Jewish rabbi and a Roman Catholic theologian. Somehow the discussion got onto the question of parish worship services. The rabbi and the priest were saying how important it is for people who live together and who have the same faith to worship together. They were affirming what I would call the neighbor concept of church and synagogue. That is, they were saying a synagogue exists to serve the people of its area, the people who belong to it.

I had to protest [against][4] the priest. I do not think churches are neighborhood phenomena, where Americans may get together with their own kind. In my tradition, the church does not exist to help and serve its own church members. The church is its members. They are the church, and as such they exist to reach out beyond themselves and to serve the suffering world. I had to say that, if any church acted as this priest suggested, then such a church had become ingrown, had become withdrawn into the lives of its own members, and therefore had violated its loyalty to God. Neighborhood churches are for people who want nothing to do with Jesus. Why? Because Jesus is on a mission. He is sent by his Father. And anyone who joins Jesus must join that mission, and must be ready to be sent beyond his own neighborhood.

After the panel session was over, I went to the lobby of the hall, and heard one girl say to another: "Wasn't that Protestant awful, the way he got angry, and spoiled the deep understanding that was growing between the rabbi and priest." That girl can be found anywhere in our society: to understand another person means to be friendly and sympathetic and tolerant of the other person's views. But is that understanding? I don't think that is understanding. I think that is the most appalling misunderstanding. That

---

[3] McGill writes here "Next page." The following paragraph is scratched out but included here. "If this is how we feel, then we cannot be sure about our love. Do we love because we want to love, or do we love—are we nice and polite and courteous and considerate of people—because we are frightened of anger? Are our hearts so filled with fear—fear of the hate that is in us and fear of the hate that may be in other people—that our love is really our way of running from hate, of keeping our hate and anger and exasperation bottled up inside of us."

[4] The manuscript reads "vs." (I think). McGill seems to use "vs." as an abbreviation for "against." In any case, I have written "against" at many points.

girl is terrified of anger. She is willing to throw away all true understanding, to suppress all real disagreements and to hide all real indignation, just for the sake of not having anger and conflict.

Think of how the parents in our communities are taught to be afraid of hating their children. They are taught that physical punishment and condemnation will hurt the child. Oh parent, bottle up your anger, your outrage, your hate! A good parent never lets loose these negative feelings.

This is absurd. Every mother has some hatred for her children. They have come out of her body, have dominated her life, and will eventually walk away. Of course she feels terrific negative emotions. But she has been taught to hide these, to fear these. She has been taught in her home to keep these suppressed.

I have a student, who comes from an Italian family where the members fully express hostility, throwing things. One evening, she has told me, she went babysitting to the house of a lawyer. When she arrived, she went to the living room with the children, while the lawyer and his wife were in the kitchen, apparently working on the dishwasher, which had broken. The wife said, "Jerry, you might pull the tray out. That would be easier." A pause. Then he said: "Dear, why don't you go into the living room. I'll get it in a moment." The children ran behind the sofa and hid— [?] "What's wrong?" "Mommy and Daddy are having a terrible fight." We just don't let our anger out.

And the same is true of our attitude toward God. Think of God as the author and ruler of all that is, the one who must bear first responsibility for this world. Certainly there is much in this world to anger and outrage us— the disappointments in our own life, the sufferings of children, the agonies of old age. No one can say, How wonderful of God that he managed events so that six children were smeared over the highway in California yesterday, or that a father in Norway was driven to suicide!

But we are afraid of our anger and hate of God. We don't dare let it come out. If we let out our anger at the world, perhaps the God of this world would get back at us. And so we bottle this anger up. We say grace at meals, telling ourselves how good God is and trying to encourage in ourselves good feelings about God.

But how is it possible to bottle up all the anger and outrage that is in us? We see news on the TV, and it keeps violating us every day in a thousand different ways. How can we bottle our feelings? Simple. We make use of Jesus. We reinforce our fear of anger by appealing to the will of God. We tell ourselves that God does not want us ever to be angry, that God wants us to deal with each other as if we had no anger and that, if we do have anger he expects us to stifle it.

And to help us avoid anger, God calls us to *be loving*. Even when we don't want to be loving, he commands to act as if we were. "Love your enemies," "pray for those who persecute you," Jesus said [Matthew 5:44]. That means, we tell ourselves, that we should always act toward others in a loving way.

In other words, we imagine that God calls us to a life of love in order to help us get through each day without anger, without hate and violence.

This command from God for us to love one another is God's way of helping us resist and repress our anger.

That is what commonly happens in our churches. And you can see how sad all this is. Is love only a way to remove anger? Is not love called forth by goodness, by needs, by the claims which others have on us? What sort of love is it that exists simply to keep us away from anger and hostility?

We here touch a point of deep sickness in our Christian churches today. This fear of anger has taken possession of love and of God. Love is how we [still?][5] ourselves against anger. It is something we use in our fear of anger. And God? We simply project our fear of anger upon God, and make him a loving God who has no anger himself, and who allows no anger in us.

In this way we project onto God our own fear of anger. As if he were some wax face that we could mold according to our whims. And what kind of worship of God results from this obsessive fear of anger? A worship of God for all the nice and good things he does for us. Do we thank him for exposing our stupidities, for breaking us in our pride, for separating us from our illusions, for judging us in our perversities? Of course not. Our God is not an angry God, an opposing God, an unmasking God.

Our God is just like us. Our God pretends there is no such thing as anger. Our God is nice, and our God wants us to worship him by realizing how nice he is. Thanksgiving, that is the worship of people who fear anger and use God as an instrument of their fear. No real and deep thanksgiving for the wrath of God. Good heavens, no. But a thanksgiving only for the good things. What of people who have starved? What is this God's relation to the children in Calcutta?

Why aren't we furious at God and exasperated for the wretchedness of so many humans? That wouldn't be nice. God doesn't want us to be angry. He certainly doesn't want us to be angry at him. Because this whole religion has no other purpose but to outlaw anger and keep it bottled up.

What can we say about this love that exists to hold back anger? Do we really love people? Or are we nice and polite and tactful and courteous, not because we love, but only because we are terrified of anger? Are we so filled

---

[5] The manuscript looks unmistakably (a dangerous word when seeking to read McGill's hand) "stell." Was "steel" intended?

with fear—fear of the hate that is in us, and fear of the hate that may be in other people—that our love has no reality of its own? It is just our way of trying to run away from hate, our way of keeping our outrage and exasperation bottled up inside of us. And is God nothing but a shadow—an empty shadow of loving niceness—which our fear of anger has created in its own image?

The great lesson of the whole Bible is absolutely clear on this matter. Hate and anger must be overcome: our hate and anger against other people, but above all, our hate and anger at God himself. But there is only one way: to let our anger into the open, where it can be wrestled with.[6]

[The following "notes" are not scratched out.] [Consider the] [l]esson of Job. Job's friends [think that if the] . . . world under God's rule violates a person . . . [then that] [p]erson must have done wrong . . . [So much for Job's] [f]riends. Job: I didn't [do wrong]. Friends: Forget what you think about your situation. Pretend that you did wrong and that God is good. Even if you don't see how this can be so, pretend it is so, convince yourself it is so. Who are you to challenge God? they said to Job. Think of yourself as always in the wrong.[7] Job: No! I shall challenge God. I shall cry out in my distress! I shall accuse God of dereliction [see, for example, Job 19:7].

Job is true, his friends are false. God can deal with Job. God cannot deal with Job's friends. They are hiding from God. Under pretense of revering God, under their love and worship and honor of God, they [are?] their fear. They do not love or honor God at all. By adopting a pose of submission, they are trying to manipulate God. Let us say that God is nice. Let us say that God

---

[6] Two-thirds of the next page of "notes" is scratched out but fairly legible—and interesting. A "word for bottled hate: resentment. Person who bottles his hate becomes full of resentment. How bottle? News on TV keeps violating us. How bottle this? *Love* is our way. Resentment—love. We keep telling ourselves that the hateful one is really good to us! Mother's day 'Don't forget how good mother is.' No one would forget. No one forgets good things. That's a silly notion. Problem is not forgetting good things. Problem is bottling up our hostility each of us has felt for our mother, to bottle up the anger which that hostility arouses in us. Whenever I hear a person being told he ought to be grateful to someone, then I wonder if there isn't a tremendous hostility that is in danger of bursting to the surface. The gratitude is emphasized, not for its own sake, but to help bottle up some anger and outrage. Thanksgiving Day. Let us remember all the good things God does. Are these gifts worthy of God? Why to us and not others? Why is God so cruel to children in Calcutta, if he's so bloody good to us? Whole emphasis on God's goodness at Thanksgiving is part of effort to keep hate and anger bottled up. As Christians, we know there is only one way to God: let this hate and anger into the open."

[7] These words resonate with—but to a quite different point—those of the title and theme of Judge William's Jutland priest friend's sermon at the end of *Either / Or, II*: "The Upbuilding That Lies in the Thought That in Relation to God We Are Always in the Wrong," Søren Kierkegaard, *Either / Or, II*, ed. and trans. by Howard V. Hong and Edna H. Hong (Princeton: Princeton University Press, 1987) 339–54.

is nice.[8] Let us focus on all the sweet things God does, and forget the starving children, the helpless schizophrenics, the cancer-sufferers. God cannot deal with people who lock themselves into their deceit, cannot lead them into the reality of the good. For they have cut themselves off from God. They do not really worship God. Their worship of God is simply their way of bottling up their hostility. Their real attitude toward God is fear and dread. That is where they really are, and that is where they must meet God. The man who throws at God his anger and despair has confidence in God to be himself in God's presence. That is faith. Jesus in Gethsemane [see Matthew 26:36–44, Mark 14:32–39]!

The Bible is clear: we are haters of God and of one another. But until we acknowledge our hate and bring it out, as long as we try to pretend that we are the righteous ones, that we are free from all hate, there can be no health in us.[9]

Consider something further. What happens when we bottle our anger? Does it really go away? Not at all. It turns into unexpressed *resentment*. And we express this resentment in indirect ways. Our resentment against this world and the God of this world: for example, my way is to wake up in the morning and not want to get up. That's how I say No to God. Not directly. I just try to withdraw from God's world. Another indirect way: we take out on our husbands or wives all that heaped up resentment at the world and at God. Most laziness is the expression of resentment. Love also. Resentment love. We love A in order to say no to B. Most of our love is resentment love. Two examples. Romantic love: Ideal man or woman—saves us from the ordinary.

Not real love for a real person. In romantic love, the other person is raised above the normal. What is the motive here? Exasperation at the littleness and griminess of everyday life. Hunger for escape. We don't rise and condemn this sordid world directly, by some vivid action. No, we express our hate of the real world by falling in love, by losing ourselves in an ideal man or woman. We do not love the real man or real woman, the one with pimples and insecurity who is slowly dying, oh no! Love is not our primary motive. Resentment is primary and we express this as love.

Another example of resentment love: Love of all mankind, love for the human race. That's silly. Love is specific. There is nothing in the New Testament about love for mankind. Emotionally it's impossible. "All humans"

---

[8] The repetition is in the manuscript.

[9] See "The Order for Daily Morning Prayer, A General Confession": "We have left undone those things which we ought to have done; And we have done those things which we ought not to have done: And there is no health in us," *The Family Prayer Book Or The Book of Common Prayer* (Philadelphia: Claxton, Remsen & Haffelfinger, 1868) 67. The phrase "And there is no health in us" disappeared from the *Book of Common Prayer* in 1979.

is an abstraction. Then why do so many humanists today love people in general? Hate for real person. Dost: BK[10]

Humanism is another form of resentment love. Fear: [I fear that] if I let my anger out, there will be too much destruction. How can I release anger constructively? That answer cannot be given ahead of time. There is no reassurance ahead of time. Let the negative out and improvise. No one can tell you ahead of time. But won't I merely destroy? That is what has been drummed into our heads. That is the view that makes us fear. No. Anger and love are not mutually exclusive; we are taught: if one, then the other vanishes. That is the lie on which fear of hostility feeds. Release anger and find out.

Jesus is quite clear in the sermon on the mount that hate must come out in the open. Go and seek forgiveness, he says, from the neighbor whom you hate. But this is not possible unless you show him really and truly how much you hate him. In Ephesians 4:25 the advice is clear: throw off falsehood and speak truth to one another ["Therefore, putting away falsehood, let every one speak the truth with his neighbor, for we are members one of another"]. If you are angry, do not let the sunset find you still nursing it.[11] In other words, be angry, but do no bottle up and nurse your anger. Thanksgivers, unless you let your God see the exasperation and outrage that you feel at the negatives of life, unless you stop making Thanksgiving a mask to hide despair and resentment, how is any movement toward authentic thanksgiving even possible? Mothers, unless you let your children see your exasperation and outrage that you feel at the way they abuse you and violate you, unless you step out of the lovy-dovy mask, again and again, and say to them—you have wounded my integrity, and for that I carry in my heart a heavy load of outrage against you, an outrage that terrifies me and shames me—unless you can be in that way before your children, how can you ask your children to forgive *you*?

[10] On a separate small sheet, McGill writes, "Dostoyevsky, *Brothers Karamazov*, II chap 4. A monk [Father Zossima] is speaking about a doctor he knew. 'This doctor was a man getting on in years, and very clever. He once spoke to me, in terribly bitter jest. "I love humanity," he said, "but I wonder at myself. The more I love humanity in general, the less I love man in particular. In my daydreaming," he said, "I have often come to making enthusiastic schemes for the service of humanity, and perhaps I might even face crucifixion if it were suddenly necessary. Yet as I know by experience, I am incapable of living in the same room with anyone for two days together. As soon as anyone is near me, his personality disturbs my self-complacency and restricts my freedom. In 24 hours I begin to hate the best of men, one because he takes too long over his dinner, another because he has a cold and keeps blowing his nose. I become hostile to people the moment they come close to me. But it always happens, the more I detest men individually, the more ardent becomes my love for humanity"''—Fyodor Dostoyevsky, *The Brothers Karamazov*, trans. Constance Garnett (New York: Modern Library, 1950), 64. (McGill is not using the Garnett translation.) See "Some Real Surprises," p. 14 above.

[11] Though McGill does not reference Ephesians 4:26, the verse is guiding his thinking: "Be angry but do not sin; do not let the sun go down on your anger . . . ."

Thanksgiving day should be a day of truth, love and anger, of anger making claims on love by being indignant about abuse and neglect; and of love making claims on anger by forgiveness. Thanksgiving Day should never become a lie of sweetness and light.

Jesus again and again speaks to us of loving in situations when we should feel anger—walking the second mile, turning the other cheek [see Matthew 5:41, 39]. But Jesus did not mean: suppress your anger and let it turn inside as poisonous resentment. Jesus meant to let your anger step forth and thus begin the work of overcoming it.

But begin, Jesus said, with God. Release your anger and outrage with him, and before him. The church is the new Israel. Israel wrestled with the angel.[12] [In what appears a later addition, McGill writes here: "Ps 39:2–4"—]

> I was dumb and silent,
> I held my peace to no avail;
>> my distress grew worse,
>> my heart become hot within me.
> As I mused, the fire burned;
>> then I spoke with my tongue:
> "Lord, let me know my end,
>> and what is the measure of my days;
>> let me know how fleeting my life is!"

So the Church took the Cross. The mark of all innocent suffering. How could God let this happen? All the children, the girls raped and mutilated, the aged neglected, all the starving and the dying are there. The Cross does not tell us what to suppress. It tells us where to begin: with our outrage at God—our anger at God. It calls us to trust God with our anger. Easter is approaching full of evasions. Do not avoid the Cross. Jesus' death is full of negatives, of rejection, hate, perversion, it confronts us and says: begin with your real self. Wherever God may take you as you wrestle with him, he cannot begin until you become honest. Let us have a little more openness about our animosity. Then—and only then—can we begin to receive and exercise our generosity.

May God bless us and keep us, may the Lord make his face to shine upon us and be gracious to us. May the Lord lift up his countenance upon us and grant us peace.

---

[12] In the wrestling, Jacob becomes Israel at the ford of the Jabbok: "Then he ['a man'] said, 'Your name shall no more be called Jacob, but Israel, for you have striven with God and with men, and have prevailed'" (Genesis 32:28; see Genesis 32:22–32).

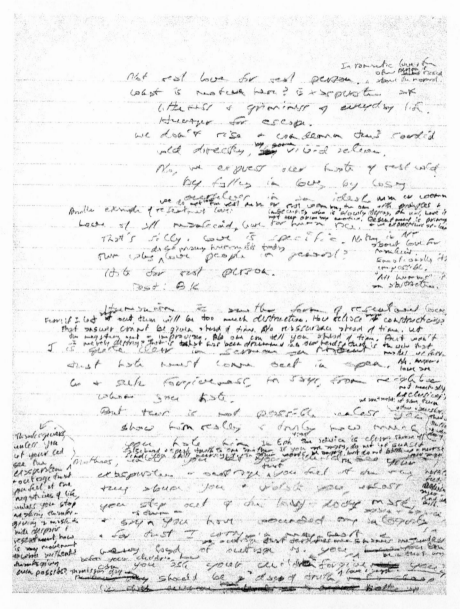

A glimpse into McGill's "workshop": an original
manuscript page from "Be Angry" (see pp. 71–73).

Palm Sunday Sermon

In truth, in very truth I tell you, a grain of wheat remains a solitary grain
unless it falls to the ground and dies. But if it dies it bears a rich harvest.
(John 12:24, NEB)

I

[Consider the] [i]rony: the crowd on Sunday versus [the crowd] on Friday.
[How] [e]asy for Jesus to be seen as a passive victim. Lesson: how barbarous
humans are. Jesus drew out the full ugliness and cruelty of human nature.
Jewish crowds, Pharisees, chief priests, Roman soldiers and Pilate, Roman
governor—all are typical of humans everywhere.

II

Danger: this is not another newspaper story about human injustice and human atrocity. That is not the Christian religion. Jesus is the actor, the agent.
He is not the unfortunate victim. For the Christian Church the day of his
death is not Bad Friday, but Good Friday.

III

Jesus' dying is his act, not an unfortunate disaster that shortened an otherwise brilliant career in religious activity. He went to Jerusalem to die. Gospel
stories make no bones. In fact, the whole New Testament takes an even more
emphatic position: Jesus' whole life is focused in his dying. In Luke, Mary
brings Jesus to the temple to be circumcised. Simeon to Mary: "This child is
destined to be a sign which men reject; and you too shall be pierced to the
heart" [Luke 2:35–35, NEB].

IV

This is very hard for us. We are a society that denies death. We do not teach our children how to die. We do not teach them to prepare for death. We teach them what we were taught: to live as if death were totally other, were only an external accident. If threatened by sickness or accident, we teach our children to do everything they can to keep death away. Preserve life! Prolong life! Protect life! That is our advice.

That is how we read the New Testament about Jesus. We imagine Jesus is just like us, full of life-projects, totally oblivious of death. He lives to enhance our lives, to help us love one another so that we can help each other to keep suffering and death away. We therefore imagine that his crucifixion and death were not part of his purpose. Good heavens, no. His death was imposed on him, against his will, by those awful people.

But as the New Testament presents Jesus, Jesus will have nothing to do with this love of life, this denial of death. He means to die. He goes to Jerusalem to be killed. He experiences this as dreadful ordeal—a physical ordeal on Friday, a grim psychic ordeal in the Garden of Gethsemane. Luke: "Father, if it be thy will, take this cup away from me. Yet not my will but thine be done" [22:42, NEB]. "In anguish of spirit he prayed the more urgently; and his sweat was like clots of blood falling to the ground [Luke 22:44, NEB]." As the reality of death approaches, Jesus' anguish becomes terrible. But it was not the anguish of being victimized by some external forces, some political evil or historical accident. His anguish was the ordeal within his own will, the ordeal of his Spirit to come to the point of taking on his death, of taking on his role and meaning as the one who was to die, his anguish was his effort of wanting to be the one he was, and the one that he was was a person commissioned to die.

He did will this and want this. He did [?] and will his own dying. Therefore I think that we do Jesus a great dishonor when we think of his death as something imposed on him against his will by Jews and Romans, when we imagine that Jesus' spirit was directed only to life-affirming acts to keep death away.

Today, Palm Sunday, is the beginning of that sequence of events in which Jesus is not a helpless victim, but in which his will, his decision, and his acceptance remain at the very center. When [Jesus was] arrested, Matthew reports how one of his disciples drew a sword. Jesus said, "Put away your sword. [. . .] Do you think that I cannot appeal to my Father, and he will at once send more than twelve legions of angels [Matthew 26:52–53]?" It is Jesus himself, his activity, his will, his purpose, his carrying through his calling—he is at the center of attention, not the cruelty of the Jews and Romans.

We today are not the first to misunderstand Jesus. For that also was true of the crowds in Jerusalem which cried out, "Hosannah! Blessed is he who comes in the name of the Lord [Mark 11:9b, RSV]!" They proclaimed him as the king of Israel, and whatever else they may have meant, they certainly thought that his role as King was to enhance their lives and to protect them from death. What else is a king for, but to preserve and maintain and enrich the life forces of a people. When this Jesus was arrested and shown to be impotent in relation to the social forces of the people's lives, the crowds withdrew their Hosannahs, and cried out "Crucify him" [Mark 15:14]. Like us, they too had no interest in a man who struggled to take upon himself his death, no interest in a man who identified his role and meaning with dying.

Like us, the crowds in Jerusalem could only see his arrest, his trial, his condemnation and his execution as a failure. He was certainly not a king, not the protector of his people against the power of death. He was merely another helpless victim of other people's destructive power.

Against this background of the crowd's quite natural view, it is no accident that the New Testament writings focus so emphatically on just that aspect of the situation which the crowd ignored—on Jesus' will to move into death. This was the prophecy of scripture. This was the will of his Father. This was the direction of his mission among people.

But how is this possible? How is it possible for any one to be free in relation to his own life? Free either to keep his life or to let it go?

In other words, this New Testament picture of Jesus going to Jerusalem with the full awareness that this entrance into Jerusalem would involve his death, this picture of Jesus coming to the point of willingly let[ting] his life be taken, in obedience to God—this picture seems like suicide. Was Jesus' entrance to Jerusalem simply an expression of a death wish? Did God direct him to self-destruction?

One of the most powerful things that goes on in Jesus Christ is that in him we have a new sense of what it means to be a human being. A human being does not have the center of reality in his life. He has his life, but he is not his life. The center of his being, his essential identity is constantly coming from God, his Father in heaven. Constantly he is receiving a very precious gift from God—he is receiving himself. We therefore cannot say that a person is his body, or that he is his biological life, or that he is his social identity. He is the child of his Father in heaven. His central being, his standpoint when he stands as an ego is a receiving himself from God. This is his essential self. In the light of Jesus Christ, then, one of the first tasks of Christian education is to teach people to think of themselves as God's creatures, as coming constantly from God. When a person asks, "Who am I?" he or she looks to God. The person [as?] being constantly made by God and given by God—this is my real self. Therefore, as this self, a person is not the same as his outer life. A person places his outer central reality, his outer basic identity at a different point: I am constantly receiving myself from God.

From that standpoint, he is free to let go of his life, not as if this were his true self, not only self, or his essential self, but as if this were something at his disposal, something he could use for himself or for others. Paul wrote, "Whether we live or whether we die we belong to the Lord" [Romans 14:8, NEB]. That is the new sense of ourselves which is given in Jesus Christ. And therefore when Jesus entered Jerusalem on this Sunday to lay down his life, he was not destroying himself. His real self, his first identity was not in his earthly life but in his Father's creative activity. That, and not his body, was his essential identity. Therefore, he disposed of his life, when he let his life go, he cried out from the Cross to his Father: "Into your hands I commend my spirit" [Luke 23:46, KJV]. At that moment, as at all moments of his existence, Jesus saw his identify as the one created and maintained by God. From that standpoint he gave away his life.

But if he were free to keep or let go of his life, if he had disposal over his life, why should he have chosen the course that he did follow? Why did he choose to let go of his life? Or, why did God commission him to lay down his life?[1]

According to our morning lesson,[2] Jesus himself gives an answer to this question. "In truth, in very truth I tell you, a grain of wheat remains a solitary grain unless it falls to the ground and dies. But if it dies it bears a rich harvest" [John 12:24, NEB].[3]

This is an example from agriculture. When a kernel of corn is put into the ground and cracks open, when, so to speak, it dies in terms of its own private identity, only then does it yield a harvest.

Astonishing.

Death is the process of communicating life to others. To take your vitality and work to convey it to others—this is a dying. It really is. It is a loss. Small [losses][4] all the time—I work with and for others and this takes my time, this takes my energy. This takes some of my vitality from me.

We must recognize clearly what this means. It means that death is not the extermination of life. It is the [mode?] of the expenditure of one's life to other beings. Death is the final [?] of the communication of life. The person

---

[1] Scratched out: "But now we ask a further question—how are we to understand Jesus' commission to die? Why should this be?"

[2] Here is warrant for treating John 12:24 as the sermon text.

[3] These words Dostoevsky chooses to preface *The Brothers Karamazov.*

[4] McGill writes "loses."

who expends his aliveness for others dies, if not today, then eventually. That is the truth. And nothing will ever change that, and, above all, the God the Father of Jesus Christ will never change that. For the whole meaning of Jesus' existence here on earth and of his teachings is just this point: to have real life is to bear fruit in the lives of others, to communicate life, and, like the corn, the only way we truly communicate life to others is by losing it ourselves, that is, by deliberately and consciously letting go of the life which is within us, so that it may pass to others.

The only real life, then, the only true life is that which produces life in others, is the life which bears a rich harvest, is the life which becomes alive, not within the person who exercises that life, but in the existence of others. In other words, the true aliveness of each human being is not to be found within himself or herself, but is to be found in those to which he or she communicates life. Jesus' death on the cross is the starkest expression of what is involved in communicating life to others: for what is involved is our dying. That is the meaning of that very puzzling teaching by Jesus: whoever holds onto his life will lose it, whoever loses his life for my sake will find it [see Matthew 10:39, RSV]. Whoever holds onto his life, keeps it within himself, never lets go of it so that it may nourish the life of others—such a person has no real life. Such a person has a sterile life, a dead life. But, on the other hand, Jesus says, whoever loses his life for my sake, that is, whoever loses his life in response to the character of aliveness that you had in me, whoever lets his life go so that it may bear fruit in others, such a person has discovered and participated in, authentic life. And therefore there is no way to enjoy authentic life except by expending oneself and eventually—or suddenly, it doesn't matter—dying.

This theme is emphasized in another of Jesus' sayings. "You know," Jesus declares, "that in the world the recognized rulers lord it over their subjects, and their great men make them feel the weight of authority. That is not the way with you. Among you, whoever wants to be great must be your servant and whoever wants to be first must be the servant of all. For the Son of Man did not come to be served, but to serve and to give up his life as a ransom for many" [Matthew 20:25–28].[5]

The life of true life is a life of communicating life. In that special sense, it is a life of serving and of dying. But the life that works to assert itself, to dominate like the lords of the world is no life at all, is dead and sterile.

It is now that we understand another word central in the New Testament—the word "love." Love is what Jesus does, and what Jesus does is to communicate life to others, by laying down his life. Love, then, is not pri-

---

[5] This passage, with variations, seems a combination of NEB and RSV translations.

marily a feeling or an attitude, though it is also a feeling and an attitude. Love is primarily an activity, any activity by which life is passed from one person to another, from one community to another. Love is the communication of life. But, since every act of communicating the life that is in us to others drains a little of life and eventually kills us, love always involves a little dying.[6] In John 15 (13): "There is no greater love than this, that a man should lay down his life for his friends [NEB]."

If Jesus' laying down his life is the fullness of love, if that is also the fullness of life, why should we bemoan Jesus' death? Was not this the full disclosure of the character of the life in him—the true life—and the decisive act of love in him—true love? With this before us, who of us can look at—or worry about—the motive of Judas or of the priests, or of the Romans or of the crowds? They are secondary. Precisely in his dying Jesus lives! Behold his life! He dies, communicating to us, conferring upon us his vitality. Of course this is *Good* Friday. Of course in his dying we see the fullness of Jesus' glory.

We see the fullness of his self-expenditure. Therefore, even in the fact of human betrayal and denial and cruelty, we rejoice on this week and on Good Friday. Therefore we also celebrate his death when we take the bread and wine in the Lord's Supper. We are not celebrating the Last Supper. We are celebrating Jesus' death. We eat the bread and drink the wine as a sign of taking his life into ourselves. In this act we are consenting to Jesus' dying, and to the fact that we too live by his self-expenditure.

And we have a lesson for our own deaths. It is a practice in Christian burial services to read an obituary. What is an obituary but the record of a two-fold love? In the life of each one of us, there is made present the life that has been communicated to each of us from all those who have nourished us. The obituary tells us of the love of all those who nourished this person, above all perhaps of this person's parents, but also of all the anonymous helpers and sustainers. That is the first love.

But the obituary is also a record of this person's life with respect to his or her dying. It tells the history of his or her self-expenditure. It declares the record of the main arenas into which that life was slowly or quickly spilled. To let our own life go so that it may bear fruit beyond us—that is the example of Jesus, that is the power of Jesus. Of that kind of living Jesus is the King, in that sense, the King of true Israel. Unlike the crowds, because we know that his entrance into Jerusalem today leads to the cross, we can sing "Hosannah! Blessings on him who comes in the name of the Lord! God bless the King of Israel" [Mark 11:9, NEB].[7]

---

[6] Scratched out here is "1st letter of John."

[7] Is this last sentence a McGillian gloss?

Eucharist

Sermon delivered 1977–1978

*For I received from the Lord what I also delivered to you, that the Lord Jesus
on the night when he was betrayed took bread, and when he had given
thanks, he broke it, and said, "This is my body which is broken for you. Do this
in remembrance of me." In the same way also the cup, after supper, saying,
"This cup is the new covenant in my blood. Do this, as often as you drink it,
in remembrance of me." For as often as you eat this bread and drink the cup,
you proclaim the Lord's death until he comes. (1 Corinthians 11: 23–26)*

Today we will have a communion service. We now believe that the earliest
record about the communion service in the history of the church is a bit by
Paul in his first letter to the Corinthians, from Chapter 11:23–26.

When we today read these words they seem a long way off. And they
seem far off, not because they were written perhaps around 45 A.D. They
seem far off because Paul sees the communion service as "proclaiming" the
Lord's death until he comes again. For Paul, as for much of the early church,
Jesus's death was the focus of celebration. And that idea of celebration is
what makes Paul's attitude seem so far away from us. This morning I want to
take a few minutes to speak about this "celebration" which has marked the
Christian Church from its very beginning.

Today it is almost impossible for us to celebrate death, because we are
taught to fear it as some kind of a dreadful evil.

Whenever we hear that someone has died, we feel a tightening within
us, a feeling of outrage and violation. We feel that way because we think of
death as some kind of alien destructiveness, that breaks into a life-system and
destroys it. We always think of death in this way. Even if the person is old
and suffering, we believe that that person's death is an unfair outrage. No one
should die.

Most of us are given images of death that help us to think of death in this way. Death, we believe, involves being broken or diseased or ravaged. Today we always image it to ourselves as a violation, an invasion, a disruption of someone's life-system. Properly and ideally speaking, each of us should never die.

We need a term to characterize how we think of death. For we obviously do not think of death as a "sleep," or as a "journey," or as a "change." Of course, not everyone is killed in an automobile accident, although many of us here have known someone killed in that way. But whatever we think of death, we are more likely to think of a person being crushed or abused by death, rather than a person taking a journey or going to sleep. We think of death as if it were exactly like the destruction in an automobile accident, not as if it were something proper and natural.

The best term I know, therefore, to characterize our image of death is to call it "catastrophic mutilation."

For us death means being mutilated—by disease, or by accident, or by age. And death is always felt to be the supreme, the catastrophic mutilation. What is the worst thing that can happen to anyone? For our imaginations, most of us would answer: to die.

Now notice carefully what this means. It means that many people today can never get around to thinking much about what happens after we die. They image the process of dying in such a nightmarish way, as such a supremely dreadful mutilation, that they believe it hardly matters what, if anything, comes after dying. Dying is a thoroughly destructive process. It is a matter of being undone, radically and totally. In all honesty, what other attitude toward death is possible, with this image in our minds, except the attitudes of outrage and horror. Death is evil. Death is the supreme evil. We must always avoid it and oppose it, as best we can.

This, as I see it, is the attitude of most people today toward dying. And therefore for Paul and the early Church to celebrate Jesus's death seems totally unreal. Doesn't Jesus's horrible death on the cross stand as a permanent reminder that dying is evil? Isn't crucifixion itself one of the most dreadful kinds of mutilation that humans have devised? In Jesus's cross, do we not have confirmation for exactly the image of death which the daily press constantly imposes on our eyes?—that in dying a person is raped or strangled or burned or broken; a person is shot or hung or stabbed or poisoned?

In other words, the meaning of this way of experiencing death is absolutely clear: no one dies of themselves. If they die, it is because they are *killed*; they are violently dispossessed of their lives by something outside of them.

If today we read Paul and hear him speak of the communion service as a celebration remembering the Lord's death until the Lord comes again, it is difficult for us to imagine what that can possibly mean.

In order to begin to approach this question, let us look at what the communion service is. For the communion service as such, the taking of the bread and the wine, points us to an experience of death in which we are engaged every day, but an experience to which we do not give very much attention today.

Taking bread and wine are a matter of eating and drinking. In all eating at the animal level, some organism dies in the process of giving nourishment to another organism. To eat is a matter of the material which constitutes an organism being taken in for the life and sustenance of another organism.

Now eating, prior to the invention of synthetic foods, always involved a dying. The plant or animal which was being eaten died in the process of giving itself as nourishment to another animal. In fact, no plant or no animal could become real nourishment for another without dying. Oh, a plant could give fragrance, an animal could give amusement. But it itself could not become food unless it were killed.

In the Gospel of John this image of eating becomes a very important focus for the meaning of Jesus. There are two reasons for this.

According to the first reason, Jesus is seen as trying to give a new meaning to the idea of life. Jesus constantly emphasizes the work of generating and nourishing and helping life in others. In fact, Jesus is even more radical. Jesus insists that human aliveness should be measured entirely in terms of the life we sustain in others.

We will hear a person say: look at how much I am alive. He will swell his chest or run around the block. The poor fellow imagines that the measure of his life is to be found inside himself. Listen to my heart, examine my blood, check my brain to see how much life is in me.

Jesus will have nothing to do with that attitude. For Jesus a person's aliveness does not exist in himself or in herself. A person's aliveness exists in all the other people whose living was nourished and supported and strengthened by that person. In other words, if I ask you to look directly at me, you will not see my aliveness. Rather you will see the aliveness generated in me by my parents, my friends, my teachers and the thousands of nameless others who have extended their vitality into my existence and by which I live. My life is not just me. It is the gift constituted by a thousand others, and continually being constituted by others.

That is why I should never be "unselfish," which is what some people want to be. I myself am a gift to myself, a gift from God, from my parents and from thousands of my neighbors. How can I be so insensitive, so callous and arrogant that I do not take very great care of this gift! I am the measure of the life which others have extended to me. Of course, I am selfish and careful about myself.

On the other hand, if you want to see the measure of real life, my real aliveness, you cannot look at me. You must look at all those into whom I have extended my life, all those known and unknown others to whom aliveness has been communicated from me. For Jesus, then, life is always and exclusively a matter of communication. Life involves communicating something of ourselves—of our real selves—into the lives of others.

Life is self-communication, the communication of the energy, or the effort or the wisdom that is ourselves. Jesus would have only contempt for philanthropy, in the sense of giving to others what we do not need—our extra pint of blood, our unneeded dollars, our surplus time.

This is not love. That is just distraction. To love is to extend to others what is crucial for our life, but something which others need in a crucial way. If you do not give what you need, you are not being vital or alive. You are giving but not giving what has become crucial to yourself. You are simply playing games. Life is a matter of real *self* giving and self-communication.

That is one reason why eating is such a central image, not just for Jesus's own way of existing, but for what life means in the sphere of Jesus. Life means to generate and nourish life in the lives of others. To be food and drink in the lives of others, and to be in ourselves a receiving—a grateful and unashamed receiving—from the life of others.

There is a second reason for emphasizing eating, and this brings us decisively to the theme of death. In the horizons set by Jesus, loving as self-communication means self-expenditure, means death. That is to say, death is not a matter of being invaded by some alien force or hostile energy. Death is always and inevitably the consequence of expending yourself into the lives of others.

If you love, you will be used up. If you extend your aliveness into the lives of others, you will thereby become tired or disheartened or confused or sick. You will be brought to the position of having to receive, of having to claim help from others. Of course, for the rich person who never gives away what he needs, who only gives away what he does not need, for the rich person giving does not bring danger or exhaustion or sickness. For that person giving means nothing at all.

Self-communication always means self-expenditure, a giving of energy or time out of the self, after which expenditure we are poorer and more vulnerable.

On this point the New Testament is absolutely clear. Jesus did not have his life taken from him by some forces outside his control. Jesus gave his life away to others. His death is the outcome of his deliberate self-expenditure to others.

Therefore, this morning when we take the bread and drink the wine, we must not try to make our eating and drinking represent Jesus's dying. That is not at all the point. On the contrary, Jesus's dying is our nourishment. Jesus's whole life was a continual self-expending to us. Death is the capstone of his giving, because his giving is not the giving of surplus wealth, but his self-giving and his self-expending, his self-giving and his self-expending to us. He wanted us to take in his aliveness and to be made alive by it, made to be able to expend into the lives of others that aliveness which he helps generate in us. Jesus wants to become our food, but the only way his life can pass from him to us is for him to die willingly and lovingly and for us to eat and drink that nourishment from him gratefully and joyfully.

Because in Jesus, death is radically [?] into an event of love, of the generation and extension of life from him to others, therefore we may celebrate it and not be horrified by it.

And the same is true with the death of our friends and loved ones. In Protestant funeral services an important role is often played by a brief survey of the dead person's life. That obituary presents us with a two-fold process of self-communication and self-expenditure; that is, a two-fold process of love in which we celebrate in faithfulness to Jesus.

On the one hand, as we hear the dead person's life reviewed, we hear of all the self-communication and self-expenditure that others directed to and into that person. And because we know that no one is a self-made or self-sustained person, we rejoice and praise God for this first aspect of love for all that that now dead person received during his or her whole life.

On the other hand, as we hear the dead person's life reviewed in the funeral service, we hear of all the self-communication and self-expenditure that that person directed into the lives of others. Here also we rejoice and praise God for this second aspect of love, for all that now dead person gave from himself or herself into the lives of others.

We grieve because we miss the presence of that person. But we do not only grieve. In Christ death has become the captive of all. We are meant to be to one [?] another; we are meant thankfully and joyfully to be nourished from one another, knowing that nourishment brings death. And therefore we celebrate even as we grieve. For in this perspective death has become an event in the communication of *life*, real and true life. And that is the meaning of death in the domain of Jesus.

Let us pray.

Harvard Convocation

Address given at
Harvard Convocation, ca. 1971

I

Our age is unbelievably verbal; we are immersed throughout our days in an ocean of words. In fact the power in words upon us is such a volume and from so many directions that all of us quickly learn to discard them the moment we hear them. It is impossible to take them seriously. As a result, the individual word and the individual sentence are no longer the unity of communication. To say anything it is necessary to speak a whole chapter, to unleash a flood of words torrential enough to attract attention and make an impact.

Behind this situation lies the sense that words are trite and cheap. When words are used without hesitation and without care, this means that they have lost their value. They are no longer thought to be alive with mystery and depth, to carry energies beyond our control. As Abraham Heschel says, "They are the objects of perpetual defilement."[1]

Words, then, are without power. They are not found to do anything or to effect anything. They inform us "about" the world, but they do not alter the world. They are not experienced as releasing a transforming energy into any situation. In an ordeal of terror or in a deep conflict that is about to disrupt a community, no one would seek for the one word or the one phrase, that would have the power to dispel the terror and overcome the conflict. Today this is inconceivable. The practice is rather to produce long mimeographed reports and hold endless meetings of verbal discussion. And because words are without power, the act of speech has become a curiously frustrating

[1] Abraham Joshua Heschel, *God in Search of Man* (New York: Farrar, Straus & Cudahy, 1955) 244.

and debilitating experience. To give a lecture or a sermon or a paper or a report has an unreal, impotent quality. Perhaps that is why it can be so strangely tiring. The act of speaking, in and of itself, apart from later developments is a non-act, for the words are impotent.

The defilement and emptiness of words is particularly evident in the churches. Here their production almost borders on a mania. The Vatican and The World Council of Churches in Geneva seem to devote themselves chiefly to producing statements. The general method of reaching people with the news about Jesus is to flood them with words—on the radio, by pamphlets at the door of the church, by book-reading educational programs, by weekly sermons.

But all this is a strangely flat kind of discourse. There is no reserve, no awe in the use of words in the churches. No words are holy, pregnant with energies that might shatter our existence. The mysteries of Christ, a phrase popular in the Roman Catholic world, are simply subjects of perpetual talk. Speech in the church is never dark, never in riddles. You hear sermons through the weeks and months and years, and they are no different in their basic rhetoric from a classroom lecture or a radio address. Can such sermons really serve as the center for a weekly religious celebration? Do they release such power that the act of delivering them must be surrounded and set apart by a liturgical service?

This vacuity of words is one of the conditions of our life today. But there is necessarily connected with this another development of more serious proportions. For if we belong to a world where words are impotent, we do not belong to an impotent world. On the contrary, power is everywhere. And everywhere that which is felt to be powerful is also felt to stand beyond the control of words. And this must be the case, if words are impotent.

The destructive violence of accidents is the most obvious case. There is a kind of raw enormity in the collision of speeding cars and in the utter demolition of metal and human life which results that simply obliterates speech. Around the bed of someone who has died from some disease in a hospital, communication through words may still go on. The grief and the blankness associated with such death are not altogether without words. But over the dead who are crushed within the truck, or bus or automobile, speech is inconceivable. The kind of power which is in action there and which has taken possession of these persons is so utterly beyond words, so utterly contrary to words that speech would be a mockery.

In a more positive area, the ever increasing focus on sexuality as the significant content in the love between men and women betrays the same features. Sexuality is the locus of power and ecstasy. But it does not belong *within* a pattern of shared discourse, of verbal expressions. On the contrary, it is precisely the significance of the sexual act to provide a mode of social immediacy utterly beyond the arena of talk and verbal reaching. As one folk singer puts it,

> If you want me, come to me.
> Forget my name and just be free.[2]

It is not that the sexual mode expands and intensifies the affections and the sharing which are mediated normally through words. The sexual act has a unique and almost liberating authenticity because it stands opposed to words, because it precipitates an explosive immediacy that frees us from the emptiness of talk. Everyone today is weary of abstractions, of attenuations, of wordiness, of most social life. Everyone hungers to wrestle with reality in its powerful and untamed immediacy.[3] The sexual act answers this hunger. For this reason, the normal Christian notion of marriage, where a man and a woman are bound to one another by their *word* of promise, by their *vows*, seems barren and unreal. Since words are impotent, how senseless to imagine that a vow as such has the power to hold and nourish and empower a human relationship through many years.

Turning away from the area of private life, nothing in the area of public policy is more evident than the fact that where enormous power is involved, policy and rhetoric and shared discourse seem to collapse. Consider the Vietnam War. As long as one thinks in terms of the United States following out the requirements of its treaties and acting so as to keep its words credible and preventing ruthless brutal aggression from depriving South Vietnam of its democratic freedom and climate where free speech may occur, as long as one looks at the situation in these frames of reference, the war seems to be an effort to maintain the world of verbal communication. It is simply part of a policy that entails the exchange of words—for instance treaties—and that champions the exchange of words—for casting the freedom of speech. But when one turns from this frame of reference and looks steadily at the brutal destruction of human life, the deprivation and maiming of persons, when

[2] David Blue (1941–1982), "About My Love," in *David Blue* (CD), Blue's first album.

[3] Pierre Teilhard de Chardin writes, "And now, in the very depths of the being it had invaded, the tempest of life, infinitely gentle, infinitely brutal, was murmuring to the one secret point in the soul which it had not altogether demolished:

'You called me: here I am. Driven by the Spirit far from humanity's caravan routes, you dared to venture into the untouched wilderness; grown weary of abstractions, of attenuations, of the wordiness of social life, you wanted to pit yourself against Reality entire and untamed'"— Pierre Teilhard de Chardin, *Hymn of the Universe*, trans. Gerald Vann (New York: Harper & Row, 1965) 60. McGill's reference is "(de Chardin, *Hymn to Universe*, p. 60)."

one thinks of the bombs and the napalm in their actuality of destructive power, these policies make no sense at all. There is simply this devastation which stands so far beyond the reach of discourse and discussible policy that it seems false even to think in such terms. Those conducting the war have shown no capacity to explain its purpose. Those who oppose the war are so filled with revulsion and horror that they, too, seem incapable of formulating policy that makes practical sense.

It seems to me that the problem of policy in regard to the Vietnam War does not arise primarily from the peculiarities of that situation. It has to do with the general conviction in American life today that when real power is unleashed, we are beyond the realm of speech. For that reason, I would expect that if we were to become embroiled in Czechoslovakia or in the Middle East in a war of savage destruction, we would find ourselves burdened by the same anguish.

Again, the same pattern appears in the present conflict over the issue of law and order. There are those who would help the oppressed peoples by changing or eliminating the social structures that are crushing them. There are the others who would defend the social structures because of their power to hold back chaos and anarchy. Each group sees the other as an agent of violence, of destructive power. The one group can never forget the police days at Selma[4] or the police in Chicago.[5] And the other group can never forget the photographs of the bodies in Watts[6] or the blacks coming out of the Cornell administration building with guns.[7] Because of these acts of destructive power, each group cannot help but look upon the other beyond the reach of discourse. For those seeking to help the oppressed, the forces of the economic, academic and police establishment seem blind and grotesquely inhuman. How can they be so insensitive as not to see the brutal consequences of their use of power? Those seeking to preserve the shelter of the present social fabric look upon the protector and rioter as utterly anti-social, as somehow perverse and blind to an indispensable good in life. The breakdown of discourse here is not a deliberate tactical move by either group. It is a necessity imposed on both groups by the violent and humanly destructive power they have seen in the other group. It is the presence of that power that, for each group, makes the other seem inhuman, anti-human and therefore beyond the reach of dis-

---

[4] "Bloody Sunday," 7 March, 1965, regarding the Selma to Montgomery marches.

[5] McGill is referring, presumably, to riots in Chicago in the late 1960s, prompted in part by the assassination of Martin Luther King, Jr.

[6] August, 1965, Watts, Los Angeles.

[7] Willard Straight Hall, Cornell University, Ithaca, New York, 20 April, 1969.

course. Violent power is the only mode of significant contact left, "Bring on the National Guard," or "Burn, Asbury, Burn!"[8]

Finally, let me remind you of a different area, that is of the strange power of institutions in our society. Institutions consist of a hierarchical network of officials. All the decisions and actions of an institution are the work of this bureaucracy. And there can be no question but that this bureaucracy proceeds almost entirely with words. Memos, reports, committee meetings—and now all this translated into the language of computers—fills every corner of our institutions. Yet curiously enough, in spite of all this verbiage, institutions seem to be directed in their overall life by a momentum or a direct energy that is never named and that seems to move the total work of all the bureaucracy in a way quite beyond the intention of any individual official. It is as if while they move from desk to desk within an office, no one can understand or articulate the overall direction. As a result, the overall momentum in an institution is peculiarly indifferent to the personal dimension of human life. It is not deliberately inhuman, just oblivious and unconnected. Every person, when he acts in a bureaucracy and becomes an official, finds that his work and his acts are necessarily abstracted from his own personal center. But this is experienced most forcefully in the way institutions make policy and make decisions. For the committee meeting is one of the most extraordinary phenomena of our day. One only has to sit through a long meeting and watch carefully how decisions are reached to realize the insidious but overwhelming power of this institutional momentum, which is never verbalized but on which every committee member relies to overcome the personal conflicts and to bring consensus out of the morass of viewpoints and words.

Of course, it is popular to identify an institution with its nominal leader and to see its intentions as the expression of his personal will. The Chicago police express the will of Mayor Daley.[9] Chase Manhattan policy is David Rockefeller.[10] The student upheavals in Europe are the work of four specific Americans. And so forth. But in institutions, no one is quite responsible.

---

[8] In an interview, 18 October, 1999, Julia DeCesare Rifici, long-time resident of Asbury Park, New Jersey, recalled, "I remember when the town was burning, and we couldn't get home. I had to go way out of my way to get back to my home, which was on Stule Avenue in Ashbury Park, because the police and the FBI agents were all over town while the town was burning on Springwood Avenue. . . . It must have been at least forty years ago. So I would say 1969, but it could have been later than that. Because I know that some of the stores that were on Springwood Avenue are not there anymore, because they burned"—*Remembering the 20th Century: An Oral History of Monmouth County*, Flora T. Higgins, Project Coordinator, Monmouth County Library, Manalapan, New Jersey, 2001.

[9] Richard Joseph Daley was mayor of Chicago, 1955–1976.

[10] Rockefeller was chair and chief executive of Chase Manhattan Bank from 1969 to 1980 (continuing as chair until 1981).

No human self-consciousness, no discussible policy at all is at the center. Decisions are made, a direction is followed and no one is quite sure how or why it happened. New York City government is only a very visible display of the situation everywhere.

The failure—or better, the absence—of words at the center of institutional life and power means the collapse of the expert.[11] For it was the expert—the most self-conscious more refined and probing user of words—who was counted on to bring words into the center of institutional life, and to inform the hardest questions and deepest directions there with discussible policy. Yet today we see that the universities—those citadels of carefully refined and expertly sharpened discourse—are just as unknowing and just as helpless in the face of their own overall momentum as the government of New York City. The experts, as the bearers of words, have failed. The power which we meet in institutions is not explosive and violent like war, though it may very well prove to be so in some of its effects. It is insidious and hardly perceptible. But it is real power precisely because it exceeds the reach of words.

I have given this rather random sampling of power experiences to indicate one point: if in our experience words are without power, it is also true that power—real power—is beyond words. The two conditions are inseparable. Real power, precisely insofar as *because* it is real power, *must* exceed the reach of words, because words are impotent. If we could find speech for the victims of the automobile accident, for the experience of sexual communion, for a policy for the Vietnam War, for the opening of discourse between champions of order and champions of justice, or for the pervasive direction of institutions, then that would only mean that such situations were without real power. It is not simply that words stop in the presence of power. Rather it is felt that power can demonstrate and vindicate its powerfulness only by showing its capacity to surpass and abolish the control of words. There any power that is an instrument or policy or a creature of human discourse is no power at all. In the face of social upheavals, to call out—"Let us reason together" [see Isaiah 1:18a]—therefore becomes a pathetic irrelevance.

II

What we have here is an absolutely central theological issue. The question of the gods is nothing else but the question of power. What are the real life and death-giving powers over our existence? What is the nerve of all religious activity? On the one hand, speech is a necessary ingredient in human existence, in the humanity of human life. For speech enables human life to be social

---

[11] This is an important clue to McGill's treatment of the "expert" in "Tower Hill Graduation—Against the Expert" (Sermon 11).

and communal. By speech, men may share their awareness with one another, awareness may open to another their own inner life.

An opposition between power and words therefore means an opposition between the gods and the human. It means that if you want to be human, you must avoid the gods, you must be irreligious in the real sense—avoiding power, and domesticating every area of life into predictable routines compatible with talk.

On the contrary, this opposition also means that if you want to be religious, if you want the touch and exaltation of power, if you want its ecstasy and its way of liberating you from the wearing burden of withdrawn self-consciousness and empty talk, then you must surrender speech.

Ah Ah! Haven't we found ourselves precisely at the point where the power of Jesus Christ has its meaning? Is it not precisely the meaning of the grace of God in Jesus Christ that the fullness of power—God's power—is shown to be compatible with speech, with human community as a community of shared consciousness. As the word of God to men, does not Jesus Christ enable human speech itself to become the medium for God's power? And within the Christian Church, is it not through such speech that men become themselves bearers of God? Power which is the presence of love? Does not the good news consist in the fact that God's power, when it enters into our existence, does not shatter what is human, but perfects and exalts it, so that our humanity is transfigured into love?

In other words, is not the fusion of God's power and man's talk the decisive, the originating event for Christian faith? Finally, therefore, is it not the role of Christians and of the Christian Church to be always on the side of talk, not on the side of empty talk, but of talk as the vessel of God's power, and therefore also as the means by which one person calls another into love? Must not the Christian community always stand opposed to power that excludes speech as essentially diabolical?

To follow out this principle in this form is obviously dangerous. As stated, it seems to authorize talk without any central principle. And today it is unrestrained talk which marks the banality and vacuity of the Church. The endless flow of words, words without significant content, words thrown out in such a volume that none carry any weight, especially for the people who speak and publish them. This flow is a primary mark of irreligion in the Church. In the face of the mimeographing machine, it is impossible to affirm the value of talk as such.

The missing element is easy to identify. The power of God in Jesus Christ gives power to words, so far as they are the channel for self-giving. In the kingdom of God, it is love that is the character of authentic power.

Language becomes rich and effective, therefore, only sofar as it is a channel for genuine love.

Verbal communication is one person speaking to others, speaking himself to others. Whatever other power speech may have, it must involve the energy of self-communication. In effective speech, the speaker must extend himself, open himself, explain himself to others, put himself at their disposal. In the light of Jesus Christ, this becomes the decisive condition for powerful speech.

The talk which envelops us every day is obviously devoid of the reality of the speaker himself. It lacks human actuality. It is about something, but conveys almost nothing of the person who speaks.[12] This is the most striking emptiness. It is speech without personal presence, without self-giving. It is speech devoid of love.

All this sounds fine provided we do not look too closely at the New Testament witness to Jesus. But if we do that, we discover there a repeated and an unambiguous warning against talk, against the power of talk to be a channel of love. Reading always from the life and experience of Jesus, the New Testament directs attention to only one decisive medium where love can be powerful and productive: the medium of the deed, and not just of any deed, but of the deed whereby a person expends his vitality, his life, as it were, for another. Above all, in the light of Jesus Christ, is the expending of one's blood, one's life blood, for the sake of others. Jesus did not come to talk, but to die. It is the Word of God, not as an act of speech, but as a deed of self-expenditure and self-communication. For the deed entails what speech never entails. It implicates us as bodies, it [?] implicates our concrete actual life in the life of others. This is not deeds of love without speech. But speech as a vehicle of personal presence, lives off of the deed and out of the deed.

In the New Testament therefore there is always a warning against talk that moves out of its own momentum, of talk that is not energized by concrete acts of bodily self-expenditure. John writes, "If anyone has the world's goods and sees his brother in need, yet closes his heart against him, how does

---

[12] Place next to these words Søren Kierkegaard's explication (concerning use of pseudonyms), "But since without qualification the first prerequisite for the communication of truth is personality [not any truth but "existential truth," truth which pertains essentially to existing], since 'truth' cannot possibly be served by ventriloquism, personality has to come to the fore again.

"But in these circumstances, since the world was so corrupted by never hearing an *I*, it was impossible to begin at once with one's own *I*. So it became my task to create author-personalities and let them enter in the actuality of life in order to get people a bit accustomed to hearing discourse in the first person"—*Søren Kierkegaard's Journals and Papers*, ed. and trans. Howard V. Hong and Edna H. Hong, assisted by Gregor Malantschuk (Bloomington: Indiana University Press, 1978) 6:178, #6440 (n.d., 1849).

God's love abide in him? Little children, let us not love in word or speech, but in deed and in truth." (1 John 3:17f. [RSV]). And James says, faith—which is a state of subjective awareness that belongs to the arena of speech—faith without works is dead [see James 2:17], i.e., sterile and devoid of God's power and aliveness.

But why does speech fail? Because that is its fundamental purpose and structure. Speech is about something else, speech expresses, not ourselves, but ourselves indirectly, in terms of what we see or think, in terms of something that stands over against us. When we speak, therefore, we do not share ourselves with another. We share whatever third thing we are aware of.

And therefore speech is always a way to have relations with another person without self-expenditure. We can always hide behind the subject, behind the "what" about which we speak. That is not a corruption of pure speech, of talk which moves by its own momentum unconnected with deeds. This is the essential purpose and value of pure speech: it enables us not to be alone, without the risk—or power—of self-expenditure. The subject always veils and conceal us, always keeps us at a safe distance from the other. As a basis and medium for relations, pure speech is therefore always a lie. And it is always impotent. So Paul can insist quite emphatically that the kingdom of God is not a matter of talk but of power ["For the kingdom of God does not consist in talk but in power"—1 Corinthians 4:20].

But there is a further observation. As a technique of evasion, talk avoids self-expenditure. Structured into it, deep within it [is] an attitude of rejection and a distrust, a spite. Therefore [??] we see the tongue as a [?] fire. [??] In our culture, the [?] of [pure?] deedless talk [is] institutionalized. [I] call attention to the classroom as a place, as an atmosphere, of no deeds. [The aim is to] withdraw from the [?] of existence. Speech [is] generated by books—by speech. [There is] the evasion of the subject. You feel the evasion. You go in [and experience] quietness, remotion. No one confronts you, [no one] claims you. The personal presence of the teacher is ambiguous. That is the main environment for every child from five years to [?] years. [In a] world of self-sustained talk, talk about, personal presence [is] impossible. The church, too, lives by the model of the classroom.

The proper speech is the deed. Therefore to recover speech with power it is necessary to take it out of the classroom and reroot it in the realm of painful deeds.

Sermon 11

Tower Hill Graduation
—Against the Expert

And as soon as it was morning the chief priests, with the elders and scribes,
and the whole council held a consultation; and they bound Jesus and led him
away and delivered him to Pilate. And Pilate asked him, "Are you the King of the
Jews?" And he answered him, "You have said so." And the chief priests accused
him of many things. And Pilate again asked him, "Have you no answer to make?
See how many charges they bring against you." But Jesus made
no further answer, so that Pilate wondered.

Now at the feast he used to release for them one prisoner whom they asked.
And among the rebels in prison, who had committed murder in the insurrec-
tion, there was a man called Barabbas. And the crowd came up and began to
ask Pilate to do as he was wont to do for them. And he answered them, "Do you
want me to release for you the King of the Jews?" For he perceived that it was
out of envy that the chief priests had delivered him up. But the chief priests
stirred up the crowd to have him release for them Barabbas instead. And Pilate
again said to them, "Then what shall I do with the man whom you call the King
of the Jews?" And they cried out again, "Crucify him." And Pilate said to them,
"Why, what evil has he done?" But they shouted all the more, "Crucify him." So
Pilate, wishing to satisfy the crowd, released for them Barabbas; and having
scourged Jesus, he delivered him to be crucified. (Mark 15:1–15)

It is always tempting—on a lovely June day when young people complete
their school years—to speak with easy optimism, and to be enthusiastic about
the wonderful future that lies ahead for those who graduate.

But this is a service held in a Christian Church.[1] Many of you are not
Christians. Perhaps there are others here for whom the Christian faith is only
a faint childhood memory. Nevertheless I am a Christian, and as I speak to

[1] Christ Church (Episcopal), Greenville, Deleware.

97

you I am constrained by the sense of what life is that comes from Jesus Christ. I have therefore deliberately chosen the afternoon lesson from the story of the crucifixion. For us who are Christians this is always the decisive event which throws light on our human situation—on the fragileness of love, on the power of oppression, on the need for forgiveness, on the cost of integrity, on the inescapability of death. This is the kind of subject which, I think, your graduation calls us all to consider.

The passage read from the crucifixion story calls attention to a sharp contrast that is drawn between Jesus on the one hand and Pontius Pilate on the other.

The striking thing emphasized about Jesus is that he really took this crucifixion upon himself. It was a development which, in a sense, was thrust upon him, which was not deserved. As Pilate said, "I find nothing in him to support the charges."[2] Nevertheless, Jesus did not try to blame others or put up a defense. He took none of the normal steps that we all use to keep those events separate from and external to himself. On the contrary, he did just the opposite. Though these events were not his doing and were not merited by his conduct, he took them upon himself. To himself—and to others—he freely identified himself with the one who was abused, condemned and crucified. He never said—"But this is all wrong. This is a blunder. I'm not the one who should be here." In a striking image in one of the stories, he drank the cup. That is, he took these events as his own. He said, Yes—this is truly I. I will be the one they whip and curse and kill.

In striking contrast to Jesus we have Pilate, the Roman governor of the Province of Judea. Pilate was free. Pilate had final authority. Pilate's word was the law. He had the right and the power to conform the situation to what he wanted. Yet he let things happen and dissociated himself from what developed. He did not make Jesus' crucifixion his own deed, even though he authorized it. He copped out. "He seems innocent to me," he said, "but since you insist, I'll let it be done. But remember, I'm taking no blame myself. Let it be upon your heads [see Matthew 27:24]."

You are now graduating and it struck me that this might be a proper occasion to look at this very difficult question of making our actions our own. In this country eighteen is now the age when a person becomes fully adult, in a legal sense, that is, the age when a person can be held fully responsible for her or his actions, the age when a person makes every action his own or her own.

---

[2] McGill seems to be speaking for Pilate, putting words into Pilate's mouth (see below), in this case operating off of Mark 15:14a (see Matthew 27:23; Luke 23:22), John 18:38b, 19:4, and 19:6b.

The story of Jesus and Pilate is a reminder that that is silly. The normal thing is not to make our actions our own. You may have been wrestling with the question of going to college and of choosing some particular college. Was that your own desire, have you made going to college something identical with your own self—even if you aren't too keen on it—or are you just going through the motions of going to college, but your heart is not in it. You have failed to make these actions your own. I can assure you that a good many marriages and a good many jobs are entered into confusedly, externally, inauthentically. Look—a person has finished college. He or she is supposed to work, should work, is long overdue in taking on adult responsibilities. But instead of being himself, instead of identifying himself as the one who has taken some job or of refusing the job altogether, he will live like Pontius Pilate. He will take the job, but will always refuse to make that his own, to be the one he is as in that job.

I would like to remind you of this obvious fact—that the hardest—not the easiest—but the hardest thing in the world is making your actions and your sufferings your own. Don't let anyone tell you that this is something automatic that happens to you when you are eighteen. It is never automatic. Neither in the jobs you may have nor with the persons you may marry nor with the children you may bear and rear will it ever be natural or easy or automatic for you to make these really your own, to be yourselves willingly and deliberately as the one who has this particular job, lives with this particular spouse and parents these particular children.

Let me just remind you briefly of two kinds of obstacles that always keep tempting us to separate our actions and our sufferings from ourselves.

Graduation:[3] [now one is able to] leave home—legally. Take on the shaping and directing of one's own life. [Take on] personal action: acts I do that I make my own.[4]

Here is the first thing that gets in the way: community expectations. So much of our lives is letting others' expectations shape us. Porter ostracized from team. Reprimanded by Sen Baker.[5] But "moral"—[is to] coast along

[3] Here McGill moves into notes, while an attempt to turn notes into text moves into [ ]. The page begins with numbers and "sailboat rental"—which may have nothing to do with this sermon.

[4] Scratched out lines—and words—follow; and there are scratchings out within scratching out. Included here in note form is material that helps to "locate" McGill's reflection: "Just at that point you who are graduating will be touching an area of grave sickness in our society: the area [scratched out: "evasion of the sense"] of moral values. / Not common / To say: legal, [?]—illusion / Most of life is acting not as ourselves. / Obvious examples: / Marry / Job."

[5] Howard Henry Baker was a U.S. Senator from Tennessee, 1967–1985. Herbert Porter was a campaign aide to the committee to re-elect President Nixon. He was found guilty of perjuring himself in his testimony before the grand jury regarding the Watergate affair. Senator Baker

[with] social expectations. [There is] no inner depth, no taking a choice in [?] and wrestling; [there is] nothing moral about coasting along. To make honesty your own value—that is something. [Think again of] Pilate and Jesus. [The contrast is between] not being different: and being oneself. How do you not coast? Break off an engagement. Legislate to yourself. Push a project you know will be defeated. Above all, [face] failing.

Another kind of obstacle to making suffering our own: going to the expert. If in trouble, we go to someone who knows what is to be done. We give ourselves to the expert, and we do whatever he tells us to do. You have all been carefully trained in how to adopt the proper submissive obedience to the expert. Mother: Take you medicine, as the Doctor said. You should get power drain out, as Mr. Coates has said.

Here is a very dangerous situation: in times of crisis, in times of trouble and hurt, i.e., just at the times when our power and self-deepening can grow most vigorously, just then we are taught to cease taking any responsibility for ourselves, cease taking our suffering upon ourselves.

Here we touch a very serious crisis in our life in the United States. By being trained to refer their problems to an expert—to a doctor, a lawyer, a [psychiatrist?][6]—now people have come to expect impossible things from technical institutions. Let me give you four examples:

1. Health: The poor doctors. People burdening them with the hope for health. Drs. can treat specific ills and injuries. But health.

2. Enjoyment: Entertainment can not give joy, only distraction. No creativity. We ask the [?] experts to amuse and enthrall us.

3. Justice: [Think of] Jesus [and justice]. [Think of our] courts: [at best courts can] maintain order but not provide justice.

4. Education: [G]o to school to get educated. Impossible. Education is the [bringing?] out of one's own potentialities. Schools cannot do that; school is too artificial a place. Life does that. Schools can only train you, not educate you. You who graduate: when your schooling is not[?7] over your education begins.

This is a serious crisis in American life. We are trained to deliver ourselves to experts.

---

was vice-chairman of the Senate Watergate committee. After learning about Porter, Baker is reported to have said, "The greatest disservice that a man can do to the President of the United States would be to abnegate his conscience" (1974).

[6] McGill has "psyh" (I think).

[7] McGill writes "not"—which does not seem right.

But when we do this, we actually ask our experts because of their specialized training to give us what we can only attain ourselves.[8]

If we look at the story about Jesus, there is one last thing to recognize. Why all this effort to make our actions and our sufferings our own? Why not be shallow, going along with the team and giving ourselves over to the expert? Why all this ordeal of integrity? Because all this is only a preparation for the real test: your death, our taking our death upon ourselves. Have you ever realized that your death is the only thing in your life that is really yours? Everything else is luck. You're not here at Tower Hill School by your own action. I'm not a Harvard professor by my action. It was luck. If I had been a year earlier or later in school, if I had not happened to hear a single lecture which got me interested in a field, if I had not once bumped into a friend at an airport—I would not be a Harvard professor.

Everything in my life is luck except one thing—my death. That no one can take from me. Jesus' taking upon himself his death is a reminder of this. Therefore, as you find yourselves wrestling with the struggle of integrity—of making your various actions and various sufferings your own, as things you willingly identify with yourself—each day you will also [be] making yourself more ready to make your death your own.

[8] In notes is this "review": "We ask dr to give us health / lawyer and court justice / the media enjoyment / schools education."

Sermon 12

On Worship

Sermon delivered at Grant Avenue Presbyterian Church
Plainfield, New Jersey
July 22, 1962

If then you have been raised with Christ, seek the things that are above, where Christ is, seated at the right hand of God. Set your minds on things that are above, not on things that are on earth. For you have died, and your life is hid with Christ in God. When Christ who is our life appears, then you also will appear with him in glory.

Put to death therefore what is earthly in you: immorality, impurity, passion, evil desire, and covetousness, which is idolatry. On account of these the wrath of God is coming. In these you once walked, when you lived in them. But now put them all away: anger, wrath, malice, slander, and foul talk from your mouth. Do not lie to one another, seeing that you have put off the old nature with its practices and have put on the new nature, which is being renewed in knowledge after the image of its creator. Here there cannot be Greek and Jew, circumcised and uncircumcised, barbarian, Scythian, slave, free man, but Christ is all, and in all.

Put on then, as God's chosen ones, holy and beloved, compassion, kindness, lowliness, meekness, and patience, forbearing one another and, if one has a complaint against another, forgiving each other; as the Lord has forgiven you, so you also must forgive. And above all these put on love, which binds everything together in perfect harmony. And let the peace of Christ rule in your hearts, to which indeed you were called in the one body. And be thankful. Let the word of Christ dwell in you richly, as you teach and admonish one another in all wisdom, and as you sing psalms and hymns and spiritual songs with thankfulness in your hearts to God. And whatever you do, in word or deed, do everything in the name of the Lord Jesus, giving thanks to God the Father through him. (Colossians 3:1–17)

I

This morning I drove from Princeton—thirty miles—to worship with you. This morning you have given up what could have been a morning at the beach, or with the newspapers, or on the golf course, or in the luxury of sleep—in order to come here. Why? What is this worship which we do? Why do it here, instead of at the beach or on the golf course?

II

If we begin to seek an answer to this question, we come to a very great embarrassment. For we cannot seem to use those main reasons which we usually hear from the pulpit. I am thinking in particular of the usual practical sermon, which presents Christianity as something that will help us arrange our lives in the world more successfully. You know the message: the benefits and value of loving others and of helping the needy. Why should we become Christians and love one another? The practical sermons give us the answer. If we do this, we shall have happier and more harmonious relations with other people. We shall be loved more by others. In addition, there will be less suffering in the world. When kindness replaces cruelty, much of human misery will be taken away. In other words, the practical value of being a Christian is that this increases love and decreases hate. In short, it brings the world closer to peace—the peace between husband and wife, between parent and child, between business and labor, between nation and nation.

III

Then, why have a worship service? If we take this practical viewpoint, we will have to say—the only practical reason for taking our time to attend this worship service is to help us love one another better.

And here is the point where I myself have great difficulty. How does a worship service help us to love one another? The sermon I can understand, for here the preacher can exhort us and instruct us to love our neighbors. But what about the hymns? What about the responsive reading? What about the invocation and the prayers?

Do these really arouse love in us—or do they usually seem so impractical, so unrelated to our love of neighbor, that they tend to put us to sleep?

Wouldn't it be better, instead of this elaborate service, to have slides about the crushing poverty in India, about the dreadful injustice to negroes in the South? Wouldn't it be a better preparation for the sermon to have a marriage counselor come and tell us about how spite and despair grow up between husband and wife, than to sing old-fashioned hymns written by our great-great grandfathers for a very different age?

The difficulty is obvious. A worship service is designed to promote the worship or reverence of God. It is not designed primarily to promote the love of people, although now and then it might also have this effect. If we want to be practical, then, if we really want to increase our love of neighbor, it would be much better not to spend our time here this morning, but for us to drive into Harlem to see the pain of the people living there, and then to begin to do something to help them.

A service to worship God is a service to *worship God*, whose ways and whom no man has seen. A service to promote our love of neighbor is a service to promote our love of neighbor, who is someone like ourselves, whose sufferings we can understand and whose needs we can try to serve.

But the two services are quite different things. That is why it is so difficult to give a practical reason for this worship service. If what we want is to increase our love for other people, there are really much better ways in which we could spend our time this morning, and much more significant roads we could have driven than the one which led to this church.

IV

If worship does not seem very practical, I am afraid we are in for an even more embarrassing discovery. There is no hint anywhere in the New Testament that Christianity is practical, that Christianity is concerned to help people love their neighbors, so that there will be less suffering and more peace on earth. Jesus never said anything like that.

On the contrary, he makes perfectly clear what a man should expect if he begins to love others in the Christian way: he should expect hate and persecution and ostracism. His Christian love will not help him to get along in the world, or to increase his friends, or to help him be nice to others or to relieve suffering, or to bring an atmosphere of peace to those around him. Know you, says Jesus, that the world will hate you, because of me. But know also, it hated me before it hated you. John 15:18 ["If the world hates you, know that it has hated me before it hated you"]; 1 John 3:13 ["Do not wonder, brethren, that the world hates you"].

The reason for this is obvious. The Christian loves his neighbor in obedience to God, because God is good, because God has commanded him to do it, and because of the beautiful creature God can make out of the neighbor.

And that makes people furious. When they discover that you are kind to them, not because of themselves, but because of God, not because of any goodness in them, but because of God's goodness, their pride is shattered and their exasperation is aroused.

The Christian does not love a person to give that person a pleasant feeling of self-importance, and so to encourage him to be nice. The Christian is not seeking the peace of this world, and the love which he learns from Christ will not give him the peace of this world.

Tell me, did the disciples who went out carrying Christ's gospel, did they improve their own peace with their neighbors or the peace of the world with their Christianity? Did they help stabilize international relations or reduce the cut-throat competition among business men or help women and slaves get a better treatment from their masters? Did they know the security of a swept hearth, or the pleasure of friends around the table and a wife singing to the children? Not at all. Theirs was a life of constant traveling and of endless work, of repeated defeats. They suffered on land and seas. They were beaten and imprisoned and tortured and killed.

Tell me, did Jesus himself achieve a happier life with the people around him by means of his love? Oh No! He was despised and insulted and hounded by the government and condemned by the good people, and finally tortured and executed as a criminal. Are we to imagine that where he failed, we can expect to be more successful? Are we to believe that, while in him this love worked not peace but the sword [see Matthew 10:34], in us it will work comfort and social friendship and family peace? Not at all. He himself tells us repeatedly that, if we take up his love, then we can only expect his fate. "Anyone who follows me," he said, "must take up his cross" (Luke 14:27). And by cross here, Jesus did not mean a velvet bed of universal kindness.

V

Then what is Christianity about, if it is not trying to get people to love each other? What did Jesus live for, if he wasn't trying to bring love and to make this world a more comfortable place to live? This brings us to what we are doing here this morning: worshipping God. For the purpose of Christianity is to follow Jesus Christ. And the purpose of Jesus Christ is to bring men a new life—the life of worshipping God, the life of loving God with all their heart and soul and strength [see Deuteronomy 6:5; see also Deuteronomy 10:12b, 11:b, 13:3b], the life of giving their wills into God's hand, the life of being the children of God.

Let us hear that again. *Life* is in worshipping God? Life is in knowing God? in obeying God? in praising God? in enjoying God? This sounds very strange indeed. Of course, it does. It is always strange, this message of Jesus, to everyone everywhere—to Peter and John, to Pilate and Caiaphas, to saints and sinners.

All men naturally believe that their life is in this world and among their families and friends. That's the only life universally known. And all men seek a God who will help their life in this world, who will help them love their families, who will help them avoid diseases, who will help their government and their land to be peaceful—in short, a God who will give them the happiness and peace of *this* world.

This is the God to whom the New York State Board of Regents was going to have all school children pray—until the Supreme Court stepped in [June, 1962]. You may remember the prayer—Almighty God, we thank thee—for what—for thy blessings. Meaning, I suppose, for food and clothing and friends and all the other things that help us have life in this world.

This is not the God of Jesus Christ, and this is not the God proclaimed and worshipped by the Christian Church. The God of Jesus Christ is the God who gives Himself to men as their life and their joy, who lets them know Him and understand Him and obey Him and rejoice in Him and share Him with each other.

The God who is good to us by helping us live in this world, who gives us food and medicine, as means to life, is a contemptible weak and worthless God, compared to the God of Jesus Christ. For everything that God gives us does not really give us life: it only fattens us for death. It only provides a temporary moment of comfort, and it only increases the wreckage when death strikes.

Death means to be separated from the life which the world can give—from the life of the body, from the life of the mind, from the life with other people, friends and family. And death is what shows that the God who helps us secure life in this world is not a powerful God and is not a good God. On the contrary, by pretending that these things which he gives are good and full of life, he is a liar—the arch liar. You remember in the New Testament who it was that offered Jesus all the things of this world? It was Satan [see Matthew 4:8–10, Luke 4:5–8]. And you remember who it was that nourished Jesus with an eternal and everlasting life, even while stripping him of all the things in this world? It was our God and Our Father in heaven. You can also understand why many Christians were not disturbed when the Supreme Court prevented the State of New York from forcing children to pray to the Satanic God who gives them food and toys and proceeds to make them comfortable in this world.

Worship God, know God, obey God, proclaim God, adore God—that is the absolutely new life which Jesus brings. And because that life is rich and full and unthreatened, in it we can find peace and honesty and kindness with each other. We do not need to fight with each other, as we do over the worldly kinds of life. We don't need to deceive each other, because we no longer depend on other people's opinions of us.

Well, then, has everything been said? Here we all are, called away from the world and the things of mammon, called to a new life in God and with God, called to an eternal life that does not depend on the world, or on food, or on medicines, or on our families, or on our sweethearts or on our children, a life therefore that death cannot touch.

But one thing is still missing. Now that we are here, what do we do? Who has seen God and can tell us about him? How do we go about worshipping and enjoying him? Where is he? In the pine trees? In the American way of life? In the things of this world? Obviously not. All those are subject to death, are weak and ultimately lifeless.

Now that we here on Sunday morning have come from Princeton, as I have, or other places, what do we do? How do we do our worshipping and how have our life? The answer is clear on every page of the New Testament: through Jesus Christ our Lord.

We, of ourselves, *do not worship God.* We cannot. Who of you knows God so purely and sees God so clearly that he can let go of the world—free himself from all the life of this world? Jesus puts it clearly: "No one has seen the Father except Him who has come down from the Father" (John 6:46).[1] That is Jesus.

We do not worship of ourselves. He worships, on the cross he showed us his self-offering to God. But he ascended and now on the right hand of the Father maintains a perpetual adoration of God the Father. *That* is how we worship. He worships in our place and gathers us up into his worshipping.

The same is true with knowing God. We don't. He does, and we share in his knowing. We don't obey God. He obeys and that is enough, more than enough for us, for me and you and all the other human beings since the beginning of time. His obeying covers us, and day and night we confess our sins without fear, knowing that his obedience more than covers them and holds us in all our waywardness. Jesus, you see, is our Lord after all. And we do not take a step with God, except in him and through him. It is in Him and only in Him that we live with God and have eternal life.

Do we live by worship? Yes, but not by our own worship. For we have a mediator with God, even Jesus Christ our Lord. Our life is to not [?] worship [by] ourselves, but is a share in His worshipping, to be made alive by the life that is in Him. Our life, as Paul says, is in Christ.

---

[1]   McGill has "(Jn 6:47)." I find no translation match.

So what did we do here this morning? Nothing practical, nothing to improve our life in and with the world. We have sung, we have prayed, we have praised, we have confessed, we have proclaimed—but all in the name of Jesus Christ, which is our way of saying that this has been all done by Christ Himself for us, and by us only in Christ. Therefore, it is not what happened here in this room which is our worship. Our worship is what is happening between the ascended Jesus and God the Father in the heavenly realm. Though we act and speak and sing here, our worship this morning, our worship that is our joy and life has been hidden with Christ in God, and has been done by Christ to God, for our sakes.

Let me read again the lesson from Paul's letter to the Colossians.[2]

> If then you have been raised with Christ, seek the things that are above, where Christ is, seated at the right hand of God. Set your minds on things that are above, not on things that are on earth. For you have died, and your life is hid with Christ in God. . . .
>
> Put to death therefore what is earthly in you: immorality, impurity, passion, evil desire, and covetousness, which is idolatry. . . . Do not lie to one another, seeing that you have put off the old nature with its practices . . .
>
> Put on then, as God's chosen ones, holy and beloved, compassion, kindness, lowliness, meekness, and patience . . . And above all these put on love, which binds everything together in perfect harmony. And let the peace of Christ rule in your hearts, to which indeed you were called in the one body. And be thankful. Let the word of Christ dwell in you richly, as you teach and admonish one another in all wisdom, and as you sing psalms and hymns and spiritual songs with thankfulness in your hearts to God. And whatever you do, in word or deed, do everything in the name of the Lord Jesus, giving thanks to God the Father through him. [Colossians 3:1–3, 5, 9, 12, 14–17]

■ ■ ■

Note: In connection with the sermon, we have jottings of further contributions to the worship service. They help to place McGill and his sermon—and his sermons—in a wider context of worship (McGill's order is "Offertory," prayer fragment, "Call," "Invoc," "Prayer." I have changed the order, based on the church bulletin, which, in this rare instance, is available):

[2] McGill reads selected texts—as above. He then lists "Hymns: All Hail / In Cross I Glory / Dear Lord and Father."

Call

Serve the Lord with gladness; come before his presence with singing,
Enter into his gates with thanksgiving, and into his courts with praise.
Be thankful unto him and bless his name.
For the Lord is good. His mercy is everlasting, and his truth endureth through
all generations.

Invoc[ation]

O God, who givest us not only the day for labor and the night for rest, but
also the peace of this day–grant, we beseech thee, that its quiet may be prof-
itable to us in heavenly things, and refresh and strengthen us to serve thee
joyfully in the work which thou hast given us to do, through Jesus Christ our
Lord. Receive from us now, O Lord, that prayer which thy son has taught us
to pray [No punctuation; the Lord's Prayer would of course follow.]

Prayer

1. We come in our poverty [?] tinsel dress / Cover this / Make us new in thy
   sight through Jesus Christ [no punctuation].

2. We thank thee o Lord for the strength to work, for the bread of our daily
   life. We thank thee for such friendship / for peace that has remained in
   home and nation.

3. We pray for the sick and lonely / protect them from sympathy. Give them
   courage for [?], from temptation, from [disillusion?] / for the aged, that
   great [?] and death will open eyes, thy [?] son Jesus work for children, that
   their weakness may remind us of much [no punctuation].

Offertory

Now we shall give praises to the Lord with our morning offering, remembering the words of him who died and who [?] lives for us: "It is more blessed to
give than to receive" [Acts 20:35].
    O Lord,
    We are all children of need and live in so many kinds of poverty, [breaks
off here].

III

Qualitative Hope

*—Friends, as the daily news reports to us
the pains and agonies of the whole world,
let us keep each other awake.
Let us hope not in the future,
but in the God who will [bless?] every [possible?]
with the fullness of his glory and his love.*

—Sermon 15

The Centrality of the Flesh

Sermon delivered at Brown University
February 22, 1961

So Jesus said to them, "Truly, truly, I say to you, unless you eat the flesh of the Son of man and drink his blood, you have no life in you . . ." (John 6:53)

Jesus said to them, "Truly, truly, I say to you, unless you eat the flesh of the Son of Man and drink his blood, you have no life in you." This text is a shocking reminder of the bodily character of human life, even in its relation with God. It is a good text for Lent, when too often the body is treated as something to be suppressed and dismissed.

In fact we all know that the body is a great burden, a great distress. It locates us in one place. Like every physical thing, then, our existence depends on preserving a bit of space for ourselves, on keeping every exterior force from invading that region that is ours. Our body roots us in the realm of physical change and competitive process.

It has the effect of making our life depend on food, on drink, on shelter. Its famines and compulsions drive our exasperated spirits more deeply than we care to realize. All our political and social life is subtly controlled by these primitive needs, and no society can endure which does not handle them. Our relations of love with one another, seen most clearly in family relations, seem to have stability when they give some satisfaction to our physical hungers. Even God, apparently, at least in the terms of our Scripture Lesson, loves us by feeding us.

The body is also a dense weight of pain which we carry with us. It is the point where we are not engaged in a grand project or spiritual cause, but where we exhaust ourselves in a pointless struggle against pain or fatigue. It is the place where the world plays with us and tortures us. In the book of

Job, Satan spoke of the grip with which the body's pain can hold the human spirit. Job had accepted the destruction of his possessions and his family. Of course, Satan said to the Lord, for his life a man will give up every outside thing which he possesses, "But touch his bone and his flesh, and he will curse you to your face" [Job 2:5b].

The body, too, seems to lie at our beginning and end. How do we arise? Out of an embrace of flesh, tangents of our father's pitiful lust, in midnight heat on dawnbed ease. The glory of our begetting was a twitch and gasp. And how do we end? Always through our body and with our bodies. Always because of some blocked or severed artery, or because of some disturbed chemical reaction, because of cancer in the breast or gas in the intestine or poison in the blood [?] is the door through which death enters. The body is our Achilles' heel. In fact, however, the moment of actual death is only the final outcome of subtle processes that have been going on in the body for some time.

The Roman Stoics were fond of saying that living is really a process of decay and dying. From the moment of our birth, the grip of death upon our bodies progressively increases. Every instant of life is therefore an advance of death. And when you tell people your age, you are not reporting how much life you have, but how much life you do not have, how much has been taken from you, how far death has advanced. Following this thought further, some of the ancients spoke of the flesh as the body of death which we carry with us.

All the aspects of the body which I have mentioned—its terrible limitations, in domineering hungers and compulsions and needs, its weight of pain, its orgiastic origin and mortal end—all these are known to everyone. A person may be startled to hear them mentioned out loud, but this is only because he has been accustomed to burying them in silence. It is no wonder then that men seek redemption from the body, seek a life where the body is left behind, where its grip on the self is broken, its pains anesthetized, its hungers numbed, its mortality avoided. It is also no wonder that this craving to escape the body should seize upon all sorts of religions and all sorts of enterprises as its way of salvation.

Just think of its powerful presence in the modern university. Think of its routine of life and its schedules, where the bodily hungers are satisfied but in a very quiet and subdued way. Think of the eating of meals in the university, which is not a ritual of life, but an automatic empty routine, where the menu is adequate but flat and where the mind is too preoccupied with reflection to be aware of taste, where feasts in the full sense of the word, are simply unthinkable.

Consider the professor, whose bodily urges and compulsions seem to flow with quiet smoothness, who does not flock to dances and does not indulge his palate, who does not starve his body nor over-indulge it, but simply keeps it operating at the lowest possible pitch.

Think of the abstractness of talk in the university, the way everything concrete is evaporated into theory. Think of the complete absence there of any vibrant sense of human death or any exhilaration over human birth. Can you imagine an instructor isolating a moment of time from his class hour to acknowledge the birthday of someone present? In the university no one is really thought of as being born and dying, of issuing from the opening of a womb and disappearing into the opening of a grave.

One might say that in our time the craving for escape from the body seems to have imposed itself on almost every corner of university life. To live as if the body were not there has almost become a fundamental creed, and the word "academic," in its present day meaning, catches this ideal perfectly. Even such noisome centers of animal vitality as fraternity lounges are being systematically suppressed. As for football and organized athletics, I understand that Brown itself is taking the lead in attacking that bit of zestful fleshiness.

The craving in every man for release from the body is always ready to see its fulfillment in the crucifixion and resurrection of Christ. What else is Christ's life with us but the overwhelming testimony to the anguish of flesh, to man's homelessness and pain and exhaustion unto death. What else is his resurrection but the elevation of the soul beyond the realm of flesh. What else is his good news but the knowledge that God is Spirit, that we are spirits, and that he has prepared for us a spiritual home, a kingdom, not of earth, but of heaven.

This is a familiar strand in Christianity. It carries with it a very definite conception of the Christian life, not so much as a way of worldly success or as a way of philanthropic charity, from which all men will have their bodily needs fulfilled, but as a way to otherworldliness. Christianity means to disengage the spirit from the flesh, to suppress the earthly earthy body and concentrate wholly upon the heavenly God. In other words, Lent, with its ascetic disciplines, becomes the essence of the Christian life.

Now we may scorn the shocking character of the text, "Unless you eat the flesh of the Son of Man and drink his blood, you have no life in you." Not the eating by itself, but that we should have to receive God through the medium of the body, through the medium of birth and [cup?] and death, of accident and contingency, of pain and need [is what is so shocking]. This text is only one instance of the uniform theme throughout the Old and New Testaments: man's redemption by God is not from the body but in and for the body. And this text is one reason why Lent is not a time of otherworldliness, a time to suppress the body and exalt cravings for escape, but it is a festival, and indeed, a festival of flesh.

The Ascension

Sermon delivered at St. John's College
Cambridge, England
May 18, 1969

*The end of all things is upon us, so you must lead an ordered and sober
life, given to prayer. Above all, keep you love for one another at full strength,
because love cancels innumerable sins. Be hospitable to one another
without complaining. Whatever gift each of you may have received, use it
in service to one another, like good stewards dispensing the grace of God
in its varied forms. Art you a speaker? Speak as if you uttered oracles of
God. Do you give service? Give it as in the strength which God supplies. In
all things so act that the glory may be God's through Jesus Christ; to him
belong glory and power for ever and ever. Amen.*

*My dear friends, do not be bewildered by the fiery ordeal that is upon you,
as though it were something extraordinary. It gives you a share in Christ's
sufferings, and that is cause for joy; and when his glory is revealed, your joy
will be triumphant. [1 Peter 4:7–13, NEB]*[1]

*But of that day or that hour no one knows, not even the angels in heaven,
nor the Son, but only the Father. Take heed, watch; for you do not know
when the time will come. It is like a man going on a journey, when he leaves
home and puts his servants in charge, each with his work, and commands
the doorkeeper to be on the watch. Watch therefore—for you do not know
when the master of the house will come, in the evening, or at midnight, or
at cockcrow, or in the morning—lest he come suddenly and find you asleep.
And what I say to you I say to all: Watch. [Mark 13:32–37]*[2]

---

[1] McGill writes: "1 Pet 4:7–?"; but the sermon clearly keeps company with verses 8–13.

[2] Again, McGill has but "Mark 13:32–"; I go to end of the chapter because the theme of
"Watch" is crucial.

In the lessons read this evening, we have the two themes that seem to split the Christian perspective. There is the theme in 1 Peter: neighbor love; there is the theme in Mark: Jesus's death, resurrection and ascension, and our waiting for his return. In one we have a religion of immediate action, i.e., a movement from ourselves outward. Giving, serving, working. "Speak as if you uttered the oracles of God. Give service with the strength that God supplies you." God is our movement of love. On the other hand, movement is from elsewhere to us. Jesus's death, resurrection and ascension put everything in heaven: wait his return.

These two themes stand in such tension, move in such opposite directions, and seem so poorly connected with each other that at times Christianity seems like a past echo of the quite different religions—a religion of active worldly service, and a religion of withdrawn, heaven oriented prayerful waiting.

Why the disruption, the disconnection between these two elements? The answer is obvious: the ascension.

Ascension means that the resurrected Jesus is removed. In fact, though Christians do not like to acknowledge this, the ascension means that Jesus might as well be dead. For death is separation. *That* is its obvious and overwhelming meaning. [?], transition to another world are all myths and speculations. Separation into inaccessibility—that is death.

But that is ascension too. Jesus [ascends] to heaven, to the arena of God's immediate presence. Wherever that is, it is not here. Jesus is no more available, concretely, specifically available than Socrates.

Therefore the rupture in the Christian perspective. Since Jesus is gone, do we primarily act in the manner of his way when he was here, serving the needy? Or do we primarily look for him toward heaven? Do I work for the service of my needy neighbor even to the point of laying down my life [see John 15:13], or do I look to heaven for the Jesus without whose presence all action is just so much fodder for death?

The message in 1 Peter 4 expresses a view that clearly excludes any sense of quandary or bewilderment on this point. Because we live in the light of Christ's return, the author writes, therefore we love one another. Therefore we are hospitable without complaining. Therefore we expend for the service of others whatever we have ourselves received. Therefore we maintain our way of love even though it becomes a fiery ordeal, a way of perpetual suffering.

The author is oblivious of our problem, of this tension which oppresses us between the present and the future, between our earthly neighbor and our heavenly Lord, between our loving that moves us on to death and our religious spirituality that moves us into heaven. Of all this, the author of this letter is quite oblivious.

In other words, to put it in the simplest terms, watching for the Lord's return consists in expending one's life for one's neighbor. That is how and where this watching occurs; not by spiritual withdrawal, not by a mental leap toward heaven, but by a hospitality and a service and a giving that entails suffering. Similarly all service to the neighbor that is done in Christ's name is not a result or an external consequence of one's relation to Christ. That is where and how one watches for Christ's coming. There and there only—not in heaven and not in the past—but there when love maintains its strength—the glory of Christ's future coming casts its light into our presence. There—in our experience of service—the future of Christ's return becomes visible, as it were, so that there our watching has contact, has substance, has nourishment.

What is this connection, this continuity between the glorified Jesus and the service to the neighbor? Why is the exercise of God's love by [men?] for one another in the midst of death the point of access to the victory of God's love over all death?

The answer lies in the peculiar opposition between love and death, which pervades the existence of Jesus and the faith of the New Testament. In Jesus, the power of God is the power of love, of bearing fruit in another's life. Judge them by their fruits [see Matthew 7:16, 20]. That is, so far as they are fruitful they share in the power of God and the life of God. He who abides in me is the one who bears much fruit [see John 15:5]. This bearing fruit in the lives of others constitutes the essential identity and being of men in the kingdom of God. I am what I generate in another. My giving is my being.

Thus arises the conflict between Jesus and this world, between the kingdom of God and the kingdom of evil. For in this world, identity consists in being able to draw a circle around some bit of reality and possess that bit of reality as your own and no one else's.

Your identity depends on what you have. Your identity is only as secure as your having, your possessing something. He who takes your work, takes your wife, takes your reputation, takes your life—he destroys your identity. To be is to have. To let go is to die.

We can see the absolute opposition between the kingdom of God and the kingdom of evil. For instance, letting go has just an opposite significance. In the kingdom of God, letting go to another, giving of what one has, what is essentially one's own is how one becomes real, how one shares in and [?] on God. He who does not give of himself to his friends, he who does not love is already dead.

But in the kingdom of evil, letting go to another is fatal, is an invitation to death. Death is the extreme consequence of letting go. Therefore love is not a letting go in the kingdom of evil. Love is an expression of one's having. Philanthropy is a typically evil form of love. You give what you do not need—surplus money, uncommitted time, extra blood. Thus, giving becomes grounded on having and becomes an expression of having. According to the law here, to be is to have, and to love is an action grounded on having.

Jesus's crucifixion is seen as the unambiguous disclosure of this opposition. Jesus, living by the power of God, really let go. There were no secret reservations, no stored up possessions. In terms of self-enclosed and possessive being he was totally negated. Yet in this process he remained alive in the power of giving, of letting go.

The opposition between God and evil can also be seen in terms of need. In the kingdom of evil, need is the death of inadequate possessions, an unsatisfactory having. I need because I lack. Need is the great evil. Love in the kingdom of evil seeks to remove need from the poor, seeks to give them such possessions that they are no longer needy. But in the kingdom of God need is the ground of love. Need is what makes giving authentic and significant. It is the soil of life. To give is to lose, to become needy and therefore to call forth giving from another. And to give to another is to satisfy his need but not to remove it. It will be there tomorrow calling forth more giving. Any effort to remove another's need is really an effort to get that person off our backs, so that we do not have to bother about them anymore.

Thus death constitutes the negation of the power of God. In the kingdom of God, need is satisfied, not lacerated and exploited. It is not made the basis for destruction, but is the occasion for expenditure for love and therefore for life.[3]

So long as there is death, the power of God is not primary, is not Lord. Where there is death, there is not God's kingdom. Therefore the Christian lives under death, or rather against death. Not against death by a more secure having, but against the whole logic and metaphysics of having and of death which gives the metaphysics its proof. He lives by letting go, by doing the one suicidal act in the kingdom of evil. And he lives by the power of God in Jesus Christ, precisely in the presence of death, precisely where the power of having is most impressive, most savage, most intimidating. He who loses his life will find it [see Matthew 10:39, Luke 17:33].

A man in Christ never swerves from the way of love, of letting go in fruitfulness to another, even when the logic of evil seems to prove that letting go is not being but unbeing, is not life but death. He lives by the power of the God who establishes and nourishes need, not by the power of the God who

[3] Thus this sermon belongs back in "II. Kinds of Power, Death, and Love." For here is *a kind of death which is not deadly but lively.* I take this affirmation to be all important in McGill's understanding of the Christian faith.

victimizes, excludes and intimidates need. He lives to be fruitful, letting go of everything he receives to others.

As the author of 1 Peter expresses it: "Whatever gift you may have received, use it in service to one another" [1 Peter 4:10, NEB (close . . . but MM)]. Let go, even unto [?] death, or rather especially unto death, for thereby you witness that death is not your measure, that having is not your god, that need is not your fear, that you await a full vindication in the future of the power by which you now live. You measure the meaning of letting go by the power of Christ and not by the power of death.

Thus in his acts of service, a Christian anticipates the return of the resurrected Christ. The power there is through power which shines unclouded on the flesh of Christ. His acts are still ambiguous. They proclaim the power of love, but also the power of death, for, like Christ, by his way of loving, by his letting go he becomes the apparent victim of death. His loving leads to his dying. In this present age, the power of God is challenged. The real letting go for others involves one's depravation and being [culled?]. But the glory of love is awaited. The return of Christ is watched, but awaited and watched precisely in this ordeal of self-expending love.

In our loving of one another shines the power of Jesus's God. In our loving of one another there flashes into radiance that glory which pervades the resurrected Christ and which in its fullness is still separated from us, still located in heaven, still restricted to the immediate presence of God. This is the theme of 1 Peter and indeed of all the writers of the New Testament. Love one another for love is of God, and he who loves is born of God [see 1John 4:7]. More than that, he is the one through whom God's power becomes manifest in a world that otherwise denies him. He is the one who is the light for the whole world [see John 8:12].

And this is the meaning of Christ's ascension. This is the meaning of the disappearance and inaccessibility of the resurrected Christ. You seek the victory of life over death. Look into your self-expending love, and not elsewhere. Glory and life are not present by the meaning of the past. There is no historical moment to which we must cling as a rock in a storm, as a light in the darkness, no historical moment which recedes further and further from us each century.

At the same time glory and life are not present by flight elsewhere, by a spiritual elevation into the heaven to which Christ has gone. His ascension is not the direction of his accessibility, but the direction of his disappearance and inaccessibility. It is not a door, but a wall.

Glory and life are present, in an anticipatory way, only in the miasma of need, only where the poor are victimized and the rich are brutal, where having is power and not having is death. There one must live the power of

God and speak the word of God. There one must have faith and hope and love—there in the darkness.

Apart from living and loving inside the shadow of death—inside the shadow of intimidation, of depravation, of degradation and of deceit—the God of Jesus Christ has no meaning, no power and no relevance.

Because the resurrected Jesus has ascended, for us the light shines, not in Jesus's past resurrection and not in his present place in heaven, but in the darkness, for the light which shines in the darkness [see John 1:5] anticipates his coming here.

Paul puts it most forcibly. In his letter to the Romans at the end of the 8th chapter, he proclaims the victory that is ours through Jesus Christ. Nothing can overcome us, he says, neither persecution, nor hunger, nor nakedness, nor peril, nor sword. For we are conquerors with Christ [see Romans 8:37–39]. But where does our victory occur? In all these things—not in [?] or in heaven, but in persecution, in hunger and nakedness and peril and sword. "In all these things we are more than conquerors through him who loved us" [Romans 8:37, RSV].

It might be said that those who cling to the past act of Jesus's resurrection and those who seek a flight into heaven want too much here and now. They dislike the poverty, the religious poverty and ambiguity into which the ascension envelops us. They want to stand beyond uncertainty. But that is not possible.

The Christian cannot really separate himself in that way from the gentile, from the polytheist who looks into his own concrete existence and sees a welter of principalities and powers [see Romans 8:38], sees a whole pantheon of gods manifesting their glory in his flesh and spirit—the power of war, the power of society, the power of sexuality, the power of disease—these flash their immensity in turn. In the same manner, the Christian lives by and toward a God who is not yet fully God, exclusively God. For all his commitment to one power, the power of God's love, his body and soul, his behavior and piety also manifest the power of death.

But the Christian also cannot separate himself from the Jew whose hope and life, whose religious assurance lie in the future. As Paul says, the Christian awaits his salvation, awaits the revelation of God, awaits the manifestation of God's lordly power in and through all things, awaits the full possession of his own existence by this God [see Romans 8:19-23]. The Christian prays that God may become the God of this world, that Thy name may be hallowed, and Thy will be done here as it is in heaven [see Matthew 6:9-10, Luke 11:2]. For the Christian as for the Jew, history is only a prelude.

But because of the ascension the Christians are inexorably separated from one other group: they are separated, as Jesus emphasized again and again, from the rich, from those who now have their religious fulfillment and therefore surpass the condition of perplexity and tension. With them the Christian can have no community. In Jesus's chilling words, they already have their reward [see Matthew 6:2, 5].

Because of the ascension, because God in his full unambiguous power of glory is not accessible, because historical facts remain uncertain and world-perfecting love remains inadequate and exalted motives hide corruption, the Christian still awaits his redemption. He watches.

But because that redemption will be here in this world, because its power already shines in the darkness, where savagery is endured with compassion and suffering is shared with courage, therefore he rejoices in his waiting; for it is the basis of his serving. "Whatever gift each of you may have received, use it in service to another, like stewards dispensing the grace of God in various forms. [. . .] And be not bewildered by the fiery ordeal. [. . .] This gives you a share in Christ's suffering, which is a cause for joy" [1 Peter 4:10, 12–13, NEB].

Perhaps, the theme here could be expressed quite simply: it is not blessed to give to the poor; it is blessed to be one of the poor and in that condition to give.[4] It is not blessed to be a light in the light, but to be a light in the darkness [see John 1:5].

---

[4] See Sermon 6, p. 62.

The Goal of Our History

Sermon delivered at Cathedral Church of St. Luke
Portland, Maine
November 16, 1975

*Then the kingdom of heaven shall be compared to ten maidens who took
their lamps and went to meet the bridegroom. Five of them were foolish,
and five were wise. For when the foolish took their lamps, they took no oil
with them; but the wise took flasks of oil with their lamps. As the bridegroom was delayed, they all slumbered and slept. But at midnight there
was a cry, "Behold, the bridegroom! Come out to meet him." Then all those
maidens rose and trimmed their lamps. And the foolish said to the wise,
"Give us some of your oil, for our lamps are going out." But the wise replied,
"Perhaps there will not be enough for us and for you; go rather to the deal-
ers and buy for yourselves." And while they went to buy, the bridegroom
came, and those who were ready went in with him to the marriage feast;
and the door was shut. Afterward the other maidens came also, saying,
"Lord, lord, open to us." But he replied, "Truly, I say to you, I do not know
you." Watch therefore, for you know neither the day nor the hour.
(Matthew 25:1–13, RSV)*

*About dates and times, my friends, we need not write to you, for you know
perfectly well that the Day of the Lord comes like a thief in the night. While
they are talking of peace and security, all at once calamity is upon them,
sudden as the pangs that come upon a woman with child; and there will
be no escape. But you, my friends, are not in the dark, that the day should
overtake you like a thief. You are all children of light, children of day. We do
not belong to night or darkness, and we must not sleep like the rest, but
keep awake and sober. Sleepers sleep at night, and drunkards are drunk
at night, but we, who belong to daylight, must keep sober, armed with faith*

and love for breastplate, and the hope of salvation for helmet. For God has
not destined us to the terrors of judgement, but to the full attainment of
salvation through our Lord Jesus Christ. He died for us so that we, awake or
asleep, might live in company with him. (1 Thessalonians 5:1-10, NEB)

I

[Let us speak] [a]bout the God of our history, the goal of our history. Our goal is the perfect realizing of the Lord's will on earth as it is in heaven. God's will for us, the good which God has for all his creatures is the perfection of love, or rather, is the condition where we all can perfect our love.

In Jesus's parable, the end of our history is like the coming of the bridegroom for marriage. Between men and women marriage is the beginning of that new union of intimacy where love may grow. In Paul's first letter to the Thessalonians the end of our history is the completion of our friendship with one another—all will live in the company of Jesus. It is like a feast, in Luke, where Jesus speaks of eating and drinking in his Father's presence [see Luke 22:29–30]. Not so much the food and drink as such, as the joyful fellowship which comes to expression at the feast [is decisive].

That is the end of our history, that is the final future, for that is God's will, that is the will of God we see in Jesus's existence. Paul put it sharply: not the terrors of judgment, but the full attainment of salvation [see 1 Thessalonians 5:9, NEB]—the full attainment of peace and beauty and joy and love. Our future is the completion and perfection of everything for which Jesus died.

II

Both passages [the sermon texts above] say something else: they say that the end of our history will be totally unexpected. It will come with the suddenness of a thief in the night. A striking image. What we must understand here is that the end will not be unexpected because we have failed to read the signs of its coming. There are no signs of the coming of this goal. There will never be any clear signs of it. Why is that? Why doesn't God allow us to have hints ahead of time when the end is coming?

The end is quite different from our present. It isn't the present improved a little. All good things in our present life are riddled with care. [Consider a] child building a sandcastle and keeping the ocean back [or not]. So it is with our families. Love is filled with care. Love breeds anxiety, worry. The kingdom of God is not like this. Love there will not bring care and worry, will not always end in loss.[1]

People say: God will resurrect us and will bring us back to life again. Let's hope not. Isn't 50–60–90 years of this life enough? That would be the worst hell—to be bound to our present kind of life forever and ever. The Christian Church never teaches a return to life, a resuscitation of the [dead].[2] It teaches a resurrection to a new life in a new heaven on a new earth.

The full good which God has for us is not this present life, is not a full Thanksgiving table for some while others starve, is not loves that die and works that fail. It is very different, because it is a goodness worthy of the full love of God. It requires a new world, a new kind of existence.

That is why studying the signs in the present will tell us nothing about whether the end is close or far—nothing at all. The fullness of the good which God has for us will come quite unexpectedly, in the mystery and pulse of God's action.[3]

We do not look forward to a perfected future because we study our present situation and can read here and now the first traces of the future that will come. Not at all. We look forward with no specific hints at all, but only because we know from Jesus Christ the character of God who makes all futures.

That is hard.[4] We often feel that that is not enough. I look at my present life, at my present world. Though I have a nice house and nice clothes, under the surface of things there are dark destructive forces at work. The chasms between me and my family, me and my friends, me and my enemies are immense. They weigh on me. The poor and the oppressed keep on being exploited by my world and your world, by my life and your lives.

On some days as I look into the present, I see no way through to the day of fulfillment. I don't want to have to rely on God, I want proof here and now, in my daily life—proof of the fulfillment of God's blessed life. But that cannot be. The good which awaits us is far beyond anything we now experience. Nothing could foreshadow it.

There is no question, then, of hoping for advance signs of the final coming of God's good. I may look at my life and the world today and feel that the good is disappearing. But that does not mean that God has failed, that God

[1] These lines (notes) follow. They are scratched out but legible: "God's good for us [is] not gradual improvement on what we have now. What we now have is not worthy of God's full goodness. Better than nothing, but not worthy of God. Filled with love, filled with loss. Defend every good vs. [against] so much violation. Lose every good to [?]—separation, death."

[2] McGill writes "death."

[3] Now the text reads: "Not easy."

[4] See n. 3.

has no more good for us. God's good for us never comes with prediction, foreshadowings.

Friends,[5] the way we are related to God is by confidence in God's nature as Jesus shows it to us. Therefore, for the little things we do, ask for predictions. We ask doctors about our health; we ask economists about business [conditions?]. But for the complete fulfillment of the good which God has for us—for the complete fulfillment of our love and care and joyful fellowship—for that no predictions will ever be at all possible.

We hope for that, not because we see signs of it in the world, not because *Time Magazine* reports that things are getting better and better. We hope for that because of the love which God, who rules all futures, has shown us in and through and as Jesus Christ. As Jesus insisted in his parable, we know not the day or the hour, and yet we yearn for the time of God's fulfilling love.

Although we cannot predict, we do not stand in dumb ignorance. Not at all. We are of good cheer [see, e.g., John 16:33]. In terms of the ultimate future which God will bring, we do not know how or when. But we do know *who*—through Jesus Christ. We know the God who rules all futures. And because in Jesus Christ that God is gracious and is moving us toward love, therefore we are confident about the future we cannot predict or foresee. In short, this is to say we look to the future and contain our anxiety about the future by our trust in God, and not by a knowledge that gives us our own power to anticipate and control the future. We grasp the future by faith in God and not by our own power.

Therefore, as Paul emphasizes in the passage from Thessalonians, though the completion of God's will will come unexpectedly, we are not dismayed. We do not live in the darkness of anxious uncertainty, biting our fingernails until some great cosmic forces grind all life to extinction. We live in confidence, as children of light, awaiting the future as bearing towards us the fullness of life, the consummation of hope.

III

But now what do we do? Do we live as best we can in the present, trying to build peace and security for ourselves now, keeping up our insurance policies, measuring our future by the size of our wealth and happiness? Not at all. For in all our present what we yearn and ache for is precisely for the future we cannot foresee. Here and now for all of us the way of love is full of grief and pain. The ruptures between people, between classes, between races, between

[5] This rhetorical use of "friends" is uncharacteristic of McGill's writing and does not fit readily with the McGill I knew. Is he here echoing the NEB translation of his 1 Thessalonians text (5:1, 4)?

sexes, between generations—these are wide and deep. Who of you does not live amidst failures of love?

To live in joy for the reign of God's love, for the reign in our hearts of mutual honor and mutual comfort—this fills every moment of our lives with the cry to God, "Thy kingdom come!" [Matthew 6:10, Luke 11:2b].

But how can we keep waiting, keep hoping? If we only could guess when the end might come, couldn't we better gear ourselves to await it?

No. No. No.

Do not imagine that that would help you to hope. Each present instant in which you live is enough to propel your longing for the coming of God's will. Each moment will generate your hope, your yearning.

But remember: if you cease to hope for God's goal, if you lose interest in the final future and the realization of God's will, then, in a sense, you have died. Because then your sense of love will have died. No person can be really happy with the present. Love yearns for the good of others and for better union with others. To love at all is to want and yearn for more, is to discover the chasms and the barbarities by which love is constantly mocked. Do not ask, how can we who love also hope? Rather ask, how can we who love do anything but hope? How can we love for one moment without finding ourselves hoping for the kingdom of God?

But if you cease to hope, to live on the edge of hope, like a child alert for the coming of Christmas, then you die. Then your love grows cold. Then you become empty and foolish like the five girls in the parable who couldn't be bothered to bring some oil. Your hearts will become cold like rocks.

Remember the final words of Jesus's parable: "Keep awake." Jesus did not mean: keep awake to the present. He meant keep your hope awake, keep awake your longing for the coming of God's perfect good for us.

Friends, as the daily news reports to us the pains and agonies of the whole world, let us keep each other awake. Let us hope not in the future, but in the God who will [bless?] every [possible?] with the fullness of his glory and his love.

IV

Grace

*"The fact that men may be neighbors to one another
. . . is only the consequence of the fundamental event,
that God himself has given himself to them
in Jesus Christ as their neighbor."*

—Sermon 16

Jesus and the Myth of Neighborliness

Sermon delivered in Schwab Auditorium
The Pennsylvania State University
University Park, Pennsylvania
Sunday, February 27, 1966

But the lawyer, desiring to justify himself, said to Jesus,
"And who is my neighbor?" (Luke 10:29)

It is significant that Jesus should answer this question with a parable about traveling. For there is nothing like travel to complicate the question of our neighbor. Think for a moment of recent developments regarding travel by automobile. There are the wide super highways, the force of eight-cylinder engines, the ease of power-brakes and power-steering. These have enhanced travel, not simply for our bodies, but especially for our nerves. And the secret is simple: all these help us to keep other persons out of our way. What, for instance, are the great advantages of the super highways? Because of them we do not have to worry about the people coming toward us from the other direction. We are protected from the delay of towns, from the impudent intrusion of homes, traffic lights and pedestrians. What is the purpose of our engines with their enormous horse power? The better to pass people in other cars, to be able to leave them behind, to dismiss and forget them. Why the millions of road signs? So that we can be on our way, without having to stop and ask directions from some other person, and to remember whether he said, the third left after the second right, or the second right after the third left.

Now all this is justified because, after all, our time is precious. We have important things to do—we have to get to the station, to the appointment, to the store, to the motel by a certain time. We have only a little while for each of our friends, even less perhaps for our families. The woman who pushes a baby carriage slowly across our way, the dog staring at us quizzically from the middle of the road without moving, the stores and blind intersections—these things drain from us precious time and effort. That is why we encase ourselves in metal and rip along the pavement, protecting ourselves from other people.

With this in mind, I think that we can feel a certain sympathy for the two travelers in Jesus' story who passed by the injured man on the other side of the road. They were the priest and the Levite. In them, of course, we have a reminder of man's inhumanity to man. Therefore it is easy to think of them as cruel, deliberately brutal people. How easy to put anger in our voices when we tell our children about that priest and Levite! How easy—but also how false.

What we forget is that exactly like us these were persons of responsibility, persons with important projects. Like us, their time and effort had a special significance. For the priest and Levites were the ones who guided and expressed the desire of the Jewish people to praise the Lord. The Levite instructed the young in the ways of their faith, and helped the adults prepare for their active worship. The priest yielded up to God the offerings and the desires of the people, adoring God with as perfect a sacrifice as possible. Along with these normal functions, there gravitated to these individuals many of the social and political problems of their society.

In good conscience, could these men, habituated as they were to being caught up in serious responsibilities, turn aside from their schedule to help that single man who had been injured on the road? Must not they hurry on, in the hopes that the next, less busy passer-by could give him help? They, after all, were not themselves physicians to treat the man's injuries. Theirs was religious work. Theirs was to be the voice even of that injured man in the Tabernacle of the Lord. Can we who brook no interference on our way to the beach or to the movie, can we who want wider highways and faster cars precisely to escape the intrusion of people, can we condemn the haste of the priest and the Levite? Can we angrily denounce them for deliberate cruelty when we do everything that we can to keep people out of our way, with such slogans as "speed" and "safety"? Can we be shocked at their passing by on the other side of the road, when, instead, we put signs along our super highways which tell our needy neighbor, "If in trouble, get off the pavement!"?

There is no need to assume that it was deliberate cruelty or even selfishness which caused the priest and the Levite to pass by. It may very well have been simply the weight of preoccupation and appointments in which their lives were imbedded, the tangle of their responsibilities to God and the Jewish community. The problem of neighborly love which faces us in this parable is not to be solved by decent living and ordinary friendliness. Jewish priests were certainly decent enough, as decent, I suppose, as any of us. What Jesus examines is a knotty and terrible problem. And all that he says is that the priest and Levite passed by, whatever their reasons. From the particular view point of the wounded man on the side of the road, they did not have compassion.

The fact that these two Jewish officials were not monsters becomes even clearer if we keep in mind exactly what the Samaritan did. Listen carefully to how Jesus describes it:

> A Samaritan, as he journeyed, came to where the man was lying; and when he saw him he had compassion, and went to him and bound up his wounds, pouring on oil and wine. Then he set him on his own beast and brought him to an inn, and took care of him. On the next day he took out two denarii and gave them to the inn keeper, saying, "Take care of him; and whatever more you spend, I will repay you when I come back." (Luke 10:33–35)[1]

One thing that stands out here is the unlimited character of this Samaritan's service. As he responds to the wounded man's needs, Jesus emphasizes dramatically that there is apparently no limit to the expenditure of his own resources which he is willing to make. In order to see this, think of the Middle Eastern situation, and then observe what the Samaritan does. He goes to take care of the wounds, but he does not simply bind them up. He pours on oil and wine, which were relatively precious commodities in the Middle East. He does not stop here, however. He also takes the man to an inn. But notice what this involves. Since the wounded man must ride the animal, the Samaritan has to walk all the way. When he gets to the inn he does not leave the man there. He takes care of him, and takes care of him all night. And then the climax. In the morning he goes to the inn keeper, and not only pays his bill, but gives a carte blanche for the future: "Whatever more you spend, I will repay"—a kind of perpetual Blue Cross guarantee. Jesus makes his point perfectly clear: the odd and striking thing about the Samaritan is not just that he served the urgent needs of the wounded man, but that he does so in a completely unlimited way, far beyond what any of us would consider reasonable. The story builds this up very carefully, and with that final acceptance by the Samaritan of all later expenses, Jesus makes clear that the charity of this man embraces even the future.

---

[1] The translation has been altered slightly to give the quotation a beginning, to supply an antecedent, etc. RSV: "But a Samaritan, as he journeyed, came to where he was . . . And the next day . . ."

There is a second aspect about the Samaritan. Notice how, in Jesus's portrayal of him, he seems to let nothing control his actions except the needs of the other man. He shows no inner hesitation or inner calculation at each stage of the way, no counting of the cost and then considering whether he can afford it. As Jesus presents him, he has a sort of *single-mindedness* here, and in the New Testament this is the quality often associated with Christian service ("Slaves, obey in everything those who are your earthly masters, not with eyeservice, as men-pleasers, but in singleness of heart, fearing the Lord"— Colossians 3:22, RSV). Jesus in fact gives emphasis to this single-mindedness by making the man a Samaritan. The Samaritans, as you may know, were a group of people living about forty miles north of Jerusalem. Many centuries before Jesus' time, they had taken the Jewish faith and adopted it in their own way. Not Mount Sinai and not Jerusalem, but Mount Gerizim in Samaria was the place where God had given his commandment and law to the people, and where God was to be worshiped. Not the Jewish priest but the Samaritan priest were the true representatives [was the true representative] of God. In other words, from the Jewish point of view, the Samaritans were blasphemous in the worst way: they had taken God's gifts of revelation and had twisted it [them], arrogating to themselves the positions of being God's special representatives. In choosing a Samaritan, Jesus was intentionally selecting the most religiously offensive figure on the Jewish scene. Therefore, in speaking of the Samaritan as doing these things, it would be obvious to Jesus' hearers that the man was not acting in the hope of receiving some reward or praise for himself. He was not a member of the Jewish community, and not one who might enhance his social impressiveness by doing charity. From the viewpoint of the wounded man, the Samaritan was a blasphemer, and it would be as a blasphemer that he would probably be treated, regardless of how much charity he did. Thus, in portraying this man as a Samaritan, Jesus reinforces the impression that there is no self-interested motive at work here. The Samaritan expends himself for the wounded man, without once calculating what he can afford, and without slyly hoping for some indirect rewards to come his way. As Jesus tells us, he "had compassion" on the wounded man, and no considerations about himself seem to have entered his head.

The trouble is that we forget exactly what the Samaritan did, how unlimited was his service and single-minded his compassion. We forget his abnormality. We picture him as acting in a normal and decent manner. We liken his good deeds to the way in which we might write a cheque to CARE, or give a pint of blood to the Red Cross, or spend an hour or so a week as a volunteer orderly at the hospital. But these are all things which we *can afford*. We are giving to others what is *not* crucial for ourselves—those few dollars, that surplus pint of blood, that extra bit of time. Our life does not depend on any of these things. In all of this charity we are being shrewd and cautious about our own needs. And because we think of the Good Samaritan's charity in the same way, we do not understand the priest and the Levite at all. They seem abnormal and monstrous.

But this normal way of giving is precisely what we do not find in the Good Samaritan. At each point in the story Jesus carefully emphasizes the excessiveness of what the Samaritan does. This man is not acting with sensible caution. "What ever more you spend, I will repay you when I return," he says. Do any of us have such surplus resources to be able ever to make that statement? Certainly a member of the dispossessed and persecuted Samaritan nation did not.

And that is the point which Jesus drives home. This Samaritan does not love in comfortable accord with his own self-interest. He does not balance his service to the wounded man with a reasonable concern for himself. He seems strangely oblivious about his own needs. If we remember this, we will not be so hard on the priest and the Levite. After all, in failing to act like the Good Samaritan, they were simply being normal.

We now come to the decisive question. Why does Jesus make the Samaritan's charity so excessive and so abnormally single-minded? This brings us to the curious fact that in recent years the point of Jesus' parable has been persistently misunderstood. We have the impression that in this story Jesus is trying to show us how *we* should go about loving our neighbor. He is trying to explain what it means in practice for us to be Christians and to serve others. He is trying to teach us how to be a neighbor to other people. Certainly this is involved. After presenting the Samaritan to us, Jesus does say, "Go and do likewise" (Luke 10:37). But that is not the primary point of his story, and neither is it the main and primary problem in every day life.

In reading the parable in this way, we forget what it is that causes Jesus to tell his story. In other words, we forget the lawyer and the lawyer's question. Now the lawyer did not ask Jesus, How do I love my neighbor? How do I go about fulfilling God's command? The lawyer asks, who is my neighbor? Whom should I love? Where can I find someone—anyone—who will prove himself a neighbor to me, so that I may love him? In other words, upon being confronted by God's command to "love your neighbor as yourself," the young lawyer asks just what you and I ask every day: Who is my neighbor? Who is such a neighbor to me that I should love him as myself? I know the people around me—priests and Levites who are caught up in their lofty responsibilities, shop-keepers who give me dubious goods, doctors who burden me with heavy fees, politicians who siphon off my money, negligent husbands who are caught up in their work, and anxious wives who take all the zest and danger and excitement out of life. We all know these people because we all know ourselves, because everything in them is present in us too—self-importance, deceit, greed and cowardice. We are not perplexed about *how* to love our neighbor. The suffering and the anguish in the world is obvious enough to call forth a charitable response. We do not need Jesus' story to remind us of that. Our trouble is the one which bothers the lawyer. We can never find anyone who awakens our love. We can never find anyone who, however much they do for us, does not also give the impression that at the same time he is looking out for himself, at least to a reasonable extent. Our difficulty is not that we are full of love, and only need a little guidance from Jesus as to how we may best exercise it. Our difficulty is that we have no love, and we have no love because we have no true neighbor, no one who proves in Jesus' words to be a neighbor to us. We know human nature too well to be deceived by appearances. If God commands us to love our neighbor, where do we find him?

That is the lawyer's question. That is everyone's question. And that is the question which Jesus answers with his parable—not how, but whom do I love? Not, How can I be a neighbor to others?, but, Who is a neighbor to me? Jesus tells his story of how three different people—a priest, a Levite and a Samaritan—act toward the wounded man. In conclusion he asks, which of these three does God command the wounded man to love, when he commands the wounded man to love his neighbor? In other words, in this conclusion Jesus simply repeats the lawyer's original question in terms of his own story—not "Who is my neighbor?" but "Who is the neighbor to the wounded man?" And the lawyer gives the answer: "The one who had compassion," the Samaritan.

It seems, then, according to Jesus, that when God commands us to love our neighbor, our neighbor is not just anybody, and is certainly not a half-dead needy person on the side of the road. Our neighbor is the one who "proves" to be a neighbor, the one who is compassionate to us, the one who picks us up and pours oil and wine on our wounds, who takes us to an inn and stays with us all night, and who takes complete responsibility for any expense which we may have in the future of our recovery. According to Jesus in this parable, that is the one whom God commands us to love when he says, "You shall love your neighbor as yourself."

We no sooner read the parable in this way than we seem to be faced with an insuperable problem. If the neighbor which God commands me to love is someone who acts like a Good Samaritan, where can I find him? Certainly not among the priests and Levites of this world. The story itself is careful to indicate that. And certainly not among the real Samaritans living north of Jerusalem. Having given a rather realistic analysis of the problem of the rich man, the man of responsibility, the priest and the Levite, we must not become romantic about the poor. If the priest and the Levite are burdened by their serious duties, the poor are burdened by envy and spite and self-pity. It is not the case that we have only to move forty miles north of Jerusalem and, lo and behold, there among the real Samaritans we will find a Good Samaritan.

It seems, in other words, that the lawyer is justified. If this story is meant to describe the neighbor whom God commands him to love, then he can only conclude that he has no such neighbor. Has Jesus given us only a make-believe fiction in this figure of the Good Samaritan? Does a neighbor only exist for us in a story and in a dream, as an ideal that we imagine in our minds—an ideal of the attentive husband and self-sacrificing wife, an ideal of the perfect ruler, an ideal of the Good Samaritan?

As a way through this problem, we must remember that this is one of Jesus' parables. The parables are stories which Jesus tells to indicate something of the Kingdom of God which comes through him. The parable of the mustard seed: the Kingdom grows over night [see Matthew 13:31, Mark 4:31, Luke 13:19]. The parable of the laborers in the vineyard: people are gathered into the Kingdom, whether they work a short time or a long time [see Matthew 20:1–16]. The parable of the lord who sends his son to a country where people beat and kill him [see Matthew 21:33–46, Mark 12:1–12, Luke 20:9–19]. The parable of the prodigal son, who is received back by his father [see Luke 15:11–32]. This story of the Good Samaritan is also a parable about the Kingdom of God coming in Jesus Christ. I think if you listen to some of the features of the Good Samaritan, you can see its meaning.

First, who comes to man with help, but in a form that is offensive, so offensive in fact that he, like the Samaritan, is persecuted and has no where to lay his head [see Matthew 8:20, Luke 9:58]? Second, who, like the man in the parable, really has compassion and cries, "Father, forgive them for they know not what they do" [Luke 23:34]? Third, whose love is powerful enough in the perspective of the New Testament not just to sympathize, but to bind up wounds and to heal? Who pours oil on man's wounds? Who is the only one able to take responsibility for all of the care which men need and to protect them from all the dangers which they face? Fourth, who alone has accepted the full responsibility for men's future, for everything they do from now until the end of time? In the New Testament, who is going to "come again," and when he comes again will repay all our debts? And finally, who is put before us in the New Testament as the only example for us to follow, to go and do likewise? Who says, "I am the way, the truth, and the life" [John 14:6]? Who fulfills the law of love, that we should love our neighbor as ourselves, and fulfills it so perfectly that it is by comparison with him that we see the love-lessness in all priests and Levites of every nation and every age?

The good Samaritan is Jesus Christ. This story is indeed a parable. Like all of Jesus' other parables, it does not tell us about our human love, and how it should be. It tells us about God's love for us in Jesus Christ. It reminds us that the one who truly serves us and is our neighbor, who saves our life and therefore draws forth our love, does not wear a very reassuring appearance. He does not come with all the badges and character-recommendations that we expect. He does not come with charity shining conspicuously all over him. He does not come as a priest or a Levite. The parable warns us, not of the difficulty we face in trying to love others, but of the difficulty which all of us will have in appreciating the one who loves us and lays down his life for us [see John 15:13], namely our neighbor Jesus Christ. He alone is our true neighbor,[2] and he comes to us as a Samaritan might come to a Jew. On the surface he is simply not impressive enough to satisfy us. And yet he heals our deepest wounds and brings us the gift of eternal life. From the world's view-point, he comes in a broken and contemptible form, apparently incapable even of preserving himself. He is not powerful in terms of his own impres-siveness, as is the priest and Levite, as is the executive secretary of the United Fund or the general director of the Red Cross. He is only powerful—but supremely powerful—in the life which he gives to men, healing their human sickness and opening to them the gates of paradise. He so fully restores them that they may become his servants, and in his name be as compassionate to others as he has been to them. He so heals men that by his power they too can go and do likewise. They too can be a neighbor to others in his name.

The fact that men may be neighbors to one another, however, is only the consequence of the fundamental event, that God himself has given himself to them in Jesus Christ as their neighbor. The lawyer's question has been answered. Who is my neighbor that I should love him as myself? The Good Samaritan, Jesus Christ. He is the one whom men are commanded to love. In the face of his service, he is also the one whom men can love easily, naturally and spontaneously. And even the priest and Levite must be included here. We do not have to think of them as abnormally cruel villains. They are not Samaritans, to be sure, but the Good Samaritan may come even to them and may make them like himself.

---

[2] Though not working with the parable of the Good Samaritan but rather with a text from the Apocrypha, "Hold faith with a neighbor in his poverty, so that you may also enjoy his good times" (Sirach 22:23), Augustine writes, "Take the word 'neighbor' as meaning the name 'Christ,' and take it so in humility . . . Take him humbly and understand him as neighbor . . ."; ed. John E. Rotelle, trans. Edmund Hill, *The Works of Saint Augustine, Sermons*, II (20–50) (Brooklyn: New City, 1990) 232 (sermon 41).

The Good Samaritan

Sermon delivered in California, 1979

Beloved, let us love one another;
for love is of God, and he who loves is
born of God and knows God. (1 John 4:7)

Tonight we will concentrate on one parable of Jesus, the parable of the Good Samaritan. It is not only an interesting story, but it has some real surprises.

It begins with a lawyer asking Jesus a question which anyone would ask: "What must I do to inherit eternal life?" [Luke 10:25].

Notice the question: not "to be rewarded with eternal life," but "to inherit eternal life."

We may be puzzled by that. If we think a moment, we know that none of us can be rewarded with eternal life. None of us is perfect enough, is worthy of God enough. Eternal life comes out of God's loving us, not out of our earning it from God by our good works. In his letter to the Romans, chapter 3, Paul quotes from Psalm 14:

> There is none that doeth good, no, not one. There is none that seeketh after God. There is none that doeth good, no, not one. Their tongues have used deceit; their mouths are full of cursing and bitterness. [Romans 3:12b, 11b, 12b, 13b, 14, KJV—with slight alterations; see Psalm 14:1–3]

In quoting these words, Paul does not say: There is none that doeth good, except followers of Christ. He says that no one—no Jew, no Greek, no pagan, no Christian does good. Therefore eternal life cannot be a reward.

But why an inheritance? Why is eternal life never earned by our efforts, but only given to us as an inheritance; that is, by somebody's death? Because it is through death, through the death of Christ, that eternal life comes to us as an inheritance.

The lawyer asks his question: "What must I do to inherit eternal life?" So we realize that the lawyer does not yet understand the grace of God, that he does not have to do *anything*—he is not able to do anything—perfect enough, true enough to be worthy of this inheritance. He is a Jew, who has always lived under the law. The law requires something of us. He mistakenly believes that he must do something to inherit eternal life.

Jesus begins by answering him in Jewish terms. Jesus begins by giving him the Jewish law, as if fulfilling the law were the necessary thing *we* had to do—we ourselves—before we could inherit eternal life. If we try to earn our way to God, we fail. As Paul remarks in Romans 5: "The law entered that offense might abound" [Romans 5:20, KJV—altered]—that is, the law has [?][1] the opposite effect from what it is supposed to have. Instead of leading and provoking us to do the good, it has the effect in us of provoking us to want to do evil. Paul says in Romans 7: "Except through the law I should never have known what it is to sin. I should never have known what it is to covet, if the law had not said, 'Thou shalt not covet!' [. . .] When the law came, sin sprang into life, and I died [. . .]" [Romans 7:7b, 9b, NEB seems the nearest fit].

So the lawyer asks a wrong question: "What must I do to inherit eternal life?" The answer is: eternal life is an inheritance of Jesus's death. You don't have to do anything. Your fulfilling the law—love God and love your neighbor—is not something you do in order to earn eternal life. Fulfilling those commandments is itself eternal life. Eternal life is loving God and loving your neighbor.

But Jesus is a great teacher. He does not condemn the lawyer. He begins answering the lawyer in terms the lawyer would expect: Jesus gives the law from Deuteronomy 6: "You must love the Lord, your God, with all your heart, with all your soul, with all your strength and with all your mind, and you shall love your neighbor as yourself" [Luke 10:27, RSV].[2]

Now the lawyer was not stupid. He did not let his religion distract him from the truth.[3] Too often we think we are religious and imagine that in that way we have become worthy of God. Thus our religious belief/disbelief distracts us, blinds us from seeing how unrighteous we are, how unworthy of God, how in need of God's free and gracious love.

But not the lawyer. Confronted with the law, he felt uncomfortable. He felt threatened. Did he love God with all his heart and soul and strength and mind? Of course he didn't. Can any Christian love God with all his or

[1] Two words here look like "not us," but this makes no sense. The sense would seem to be complete in the text above.

[2] McGill is working with Luke 10:27, but see Deuteronomy 6:5.

[3] So much of McGill is in this line.

her heart and soul and strength and mind? Of course not. There is none righteous, no, not one. Did the lawyer really love his neighbor as himself? Of course he didn't. Just as Paul later wrote to the Romans, the lawyer knew that the law only had the effect of arousing him to sin.

Therefore he had to justify himself. His heart knew that before the law he could not stand. Before the law he was condemned. He felt terror. He had to justify himself. So he asks a question, as if the law were not clear, as if the law were too difficult for him to understand. The law is too difficult for him to *do*, but if he, a Jewish lawyer, says he does not understand the law, he is only trying to justify himself, to find an excuse for his not fulfilling the law.

So he asks Jesus the question: "But who is my neighbor?" [Luke 10:29b]. That is, whom does God ask me to love as myself?"

So Jesus gives the parable of the Good Samaritan. We must remember the lawyer's question, because the parable is Jesus's effort to help the man see the answer to his question, not according to the law of the old covenant, but according to the love of God.

A man on his way from Jerusalem to Jericho was attacked by robbers. The region east of Jerusalem was desert. Jericho was an affluent community. What happened when the robbers attacked the man? Jesus says that the robbers "stripped him" [Luke 10:30, RSV], i.e., stripped him of his possessions, including his clothing, "and beat him and departed, leaving him half dead" [Luke 10:30b, RSV].

These people were not just robbers who took property. They attacked the man's body. We would say that they were assaulters. In our law assault against a person's body is much more serious than robbery. The man was not merely robbed, which is bad enough. He was beaten and wounded.

Then Jesus continues his story: A priest and a Levite came by the wounded man, and "passed by on the other side" [Luke 10:31–32, RSV]. Now that's a very striking description. They passed by on the other side of the way, of the street.

Since you and I and all people have often done the same, this description strikes us all. We have all passed by on the other side. The priest and the Levite were not unusual villains; they were responsible leaders in the temple. They were probably going to Jericho, where only the wealthy priests and Levites could afford to live.

Why did they pass by on the other side, i.e., going out of their way to avoid the naked, wounded man? Jesus does not say. But you and I have only to look in ourselves in order to see there a thousand reasons for their passing by on the other side.

The reason that strikes me, especially since priests and Levites carried such responsibilities in the Jewish temple, is that these men were important and responsible, therefore busy. They lived with claims always being placed upon them. They were the kind who are busy, even when they haven't anything to do. They are always looking ahead with a schedule by which they try to cope with the many tasks awaiting them.

Could they let an unexpected victim of robbery along the road interrupt them? Aren't they too busy? Don't they have too many other responsibilities to take on this task?

I think that in the priest and the Levite Jesus is warning us not to get trapped in our duties, not to get fixed in our responsibilities. Play loose enough with your responsibilities that you can let a neighbor's need interrupt you, let it throw you off your schedule and disrupt your plans. If your plans are too important for that, if you are such a slave to your responsibilities that you think you don't have time to help a stranger fix his flat tire, to take a neighbor to the store, then you are like the priest and the Levite.

Then Jesus comes to the crucial point of his parable: After the priest and the Levite there comes along a Samaritan. Now the Samaritans were usually hated by the Jews, much as many Christians hate the Jews, and as we Americans hate the communists. The Jews thought that the Samaritans lived in an evil way. Specifically they rejected worship in the Jewish temple and instead worshiped God in their own city, far north of Jerusalem.

Jesus says that the Samaritan, then considered evil by the Jews, did not pass by on the other side. He had pity on the naked wounded man. He bound up the man's wounds, pouring on oil and wine, which were very expensive commodities in Palestine then. He set the man on his donkey, and he walked on the road all the way until they came to an inn. In short, in Jesus's words, he took care of him.

But we all know ourselves the point that Jesus is making here. If you are going to take care of someone, you are going to have to use your effort—as the Samaritan walked all the way to the inn. You are going to have to take your time—as the Samaritan let himself be guided, not by his desires or by his duties, but by what was needed to take care of the wounded man. And if you take care of someone, you will have to spend your income. Effort, time and money—that is what taking care of someone involves.

I had an operation this summer, and Brother Edward's[4] daughter, Edith, came East, gave up her time, and used her money to take care of me. That is exactly what the Samaritan did.

But that is not all. Jesus continues: The Samaritan stayed at the inn with the wounded man all night. The next morning, when he went to leave, the

---

[4] Scratched out at the beginning of the manuscript is: "Great privilege to speak / Thank Brother Edwards."

Samaritan not only paid the bill at the inn, but knowing that the wounded man was robbed of everything and might be destitute, he said to the innkeeper: "Take care of him. Whatever more you spend, I will repay you when I return" [Luke 10:35b, RSV is nearest].

This last detail shows how extraordinary is the Samaritan's care; how unstinted and unconditional. He not only gives up his time. He not only takes care of this wounded stranger a whole night. He not only pays the hotel bill up to that time. He tells the innkeeper that he will pay everything required for this stranger's recovery when he returns.

Well! That leaves us out of the picture. Are any of us willing or even able to care for someone in that way? That sounds almost irresponsible on the part of the Samaritan.

Jesus may end his parable with the command to us: Go and do as the Samaritan did. Go and let your care for others be unstinted and unrestrained, opening up for them—even for needy strangers—all your time and all your effort and all your resources.

But how awful! Has Jesus only confronted us again with the law we cannot fulfill? Are we still strapped in our unrighteousness? Has nothing changed? Does the lawyer still remain unjustified and condemned before the law? Is there no grace in the parable? How can anyone of us, "Go and do just as the Samaritan did" [see Luke 10:37b]. Who has the time? Who has the money?

In other words, I have explained details of Jesus's parable, but somehow I missed the central point of the parable, the astonishing good news of God's love and grace.

We have missed the heart of the story. We can see that center by the way Jesus turns a question to the lawyer at the end of his parable. Jesus says: "Which of these three men do you think was a neighbor to the man who fell among robbers?" [Luke 10:36, NEB is nearest].

Now that question is often overlooked. The lawyer asks Jesus: "Who is my neighbor?" Jesus tells his parable and asks, "Which of the three men was the neighbor to the wounded man?" That is, according to Jesus, our neighbor—the one God commands us to love—is not a strange victim on the side of the road, is not anyone. Our neighbor—that is, the one God commands us to love—is the man who takes care of us like the Samaritan, the man who stops on his way, binds up our wounds, takes us to an inn, and pays all our costs—that is our neighbor and therefore, that is the one we should love as ourselves.

But, we say, that's easy. If that is so, anyone could do that. Exactly. If someone cares for us, we can love him or her. That is the first surprise in

Jesus's interpretation of the law. The neighbor is not the one who lives near you. The neighbor is one who takes care of you like this Samaritan.

Remember the words in 1 John: "Here is love, not that we loved God, but that he loved us. [. . .] We love him, but because He first loved us" [4:10, 19, RSV is nearest]. Jesus in his parable is saying the same about the commandment to love our neighbor. We do not first love our neighbor, first our neighbor loves us.

Now all of us can ask the question which the lawyer first asked Jesus: "Who is my neighbor?" [Luke 10:29]. Who will take care of me in my need in this way? Not my landlord, not my banker. Not my policeman. Not my doctor. *I* have to pay them for care. *I* have to earn their care. Where can I find a good Samaritan? Where is anyone my neighbor so I can love him and fulfill God's command?

The answer is clear. Who in the New Testament is present as the one who loves us without stint? Who gives up for us, not only his time and effort and money, but who also gives up his life for us? Who is the one who will repay us all for the care we expend for others when he returns, when he comes in clouds of glory [see Matthew 24:30, Mark 13:26, Luke 21:27]? Who does the New Testament present to us as the one we should imitate in our love, the one we should follow in our action?

The good Samaritan is Jesus Christ. He is our neighbor. He is the one we should, we may, and we can love as ourselves.

Appendix 1

Confession of Faith
by Arthur C. McGill

Early Development

I was brought up in the suburbs of Boston, Massachusetts. My mother was a devout woman, and both my parents were active in the church. All during my early years I went to Sunday school, and when I joined the Congregational Church in Wellesley, Massachusetts, I continued to attend its services.

At that time I accepted the church for the values it affirmed—brotherly love, social harmony, honest and sincere living. These values were offered by the church in terms of practical self-interest; they were to be followed as the best technique for a successful life. The church's talk about God and Christ seemed to me then largely a verbal habit. This impression was strengthened by what I saw of the social life of the church, where the people's motives and conduct were the same as in normal church groups, and where, except for an occasional prayer, God was totally absent. Thus Christianity presented itself to me as an excuse for sociability. What is religion? Religion is when we go to church and worship God. What is God? God is what we worship when we go to church.

So I came to ignore the church, and by the time I was through high school I also had largely given up brotherly love as a technique for success. I had found how love and loyalty and sincerity in normal everyday social relations disturbed people; these qualities made them feel uncomfortably obligated and often aroused resentment. Politeness and easygoing amiability were far better techniques, and, like most young people, I adopted these.

When I was trying to decide upon a vocation, the adults who counseled me usually made the matter of self-realization the crucial point. Take that job, I was advised, which is best for your abilities and offers the most security. There was no mention of service, and although those who advised me may have assumed that all jobs serve, this motive was never clearly set before me.

So I entered college [Harvard] with the hope of being a theoretical physicist without any clear sense of service.

Revelation of God

While preoccupied with the math and physics at college, I came through readings in American literature, curiously enough, to the shattering apprehension of the reality of God, a sense of the actual vital existence of a being Supremely real and powerful and magnificent.

There were two aspects of my apprehension of God at this time. First, I came to see His magnificent holiness through the discovery of the utter and absolute dependence of everything upon Him.

It is very possible that my study in atomic physics contributed to this experience. I had been educated in what is often called the scientific worldview, which interprets every event as the effect of preceding observable events, and which sees the ground of our existence in basic units of matter. As you may know, however, we are now at the point in nuclear physics where the material units of existence behave in such contradictory ways that they cannot be pictured. All we can do is write mathematical equations about them. It is possible that my daily contact with this situation and my work with the nuclear machines in the laboratory tended to make the reality of matter evaporate before me.

I thus came to see all things as dependent for their minute-to-minute existence upon the sustaining power of some transcendent being. My entire understanding of nature was transformed. Instead of a causal sequence of events grounded on matter, I now apprehended a living inscrutable God, and all things were wholly in His hands.

It was in the face of this revelation that I first learned the meaning of worship. In the presence of God, of One who gives all reality its continuing existence, who chooses us, as it were, by calling us into being—before Him the heart of man spontaneously bows itself in awe and reverence and utter adoration. Religion, I thus discovered, was not a solution for personal problems; rather, it posed the most serious of problems. It certainly did not constitute being benevolent toward one's neighbor. It consisted of recognizing and worshipping the Lord of all.

At this time, in fact, I made little connection between religion and the love of neighbor.

Besides the consciousness of utter dependence and the accompanying experience of worship, this revelation had for me a second aspect: a sense of the depth and seeming hopelessness of evil, especially of human sin. If God is indeed the Lord of life, if the crucial fact of a man's existence is not his own living and his achievements, as I had been taught, but is God's creative action, then a sense of worship should be the dominant passion of a man's whole life. Yet by some unbelievable twist, man has turned his back on God, has in his conscious [conscience?] cut himself off from the source of his own vitality and strength and being. Thus I came to understand that sin is not a matter of morality or conduct, but is that state or orientation of a man's entire consciousness which does not make God its center.

At college when I felt the impact of this religious meaning of evil, the whole gamut of everyday living appeared to me as a life of sheer sin, a life of separation from God. And the thing that appalled me was the complacent attitude which the world and the church and I myself took toward this condition. We all not only accepted it, but idolized it and boasted in it as good. Wholly unable to call up in myself the devotion of worship, I, and my neighbors also, seemed to be living an existence that in its shallow self-centeredness was truly under the wrath of God. The meaning of life which my environment had taught me was, like my former view of nature, now destroyed.

My growing awareness of the reality of evil at this time made me sensitive to some of its other dimensions. I found myself confronted with the appalling reality of suffering in the lives of some people, for whom pain and frustration were not temporary accidents but were the dominant elements of their experience. I especially remember how troubled I was by a Boston beggar with a mangled face, and how I wondered what horrible image of himself he must carry with him, since all eyes that turned his way showed revulsion and disgust. In the reality of suffering I first sensed how men are in the grip of evil powers beyond them, how there is a kind of demonry in nature and history that can seize us and crush us.

My religious awareness at this time came to center on the New Testament figure of Jesus. And Jesus struck me above all, not for his love of men, but for his worship of God. In Jesus I found a man who throughout his existence recognized and honored God for what God really was—his Lord. Real devoted worship seemed to me to be the dominant passion in Jesus' life, and even his love of man appeared as a function of this. And yet in the story of Jesus I was also confronted by evil in its most intense forms. Here the hopeless sin of men separated from God destroyed the good they could not even recognize. Here even the supremely good man was subjected to suffering and isolation by the demonic powers. And here, finally, was the terrible mockery of death. I had never heard the church take the resurrection seriously, so that for me at this time the story of Jesus ended with the Cross.

Thus my whole religious consciousness—the sense of worship and of evil—found its extreme representation and contradiction in the life of Jesus.

The Revelation of Christ

The second and culminating movement in my religious experience was my encounter with the decisive fact of the Incarnation. What dawned on my mind was the realization that the belief of the gospel of John might be true. What if God, the ground of all reality, was actually, concretely, personally in Jesus of Nazareth? And what began for me as an incredible possibility came to be the focal point of my life.

The crucial thing that I found was not that Jesus knew something distinctive about God, nor that he had certain attributes like God, nor that his life was commended by God, but rather that his Person was the Person of God and therefore he was indeed the revelation of God. In Jesus' steady acceptance of men in their evil, in his constant affirming of them in the face of their indifferent cruelty and pride—here I saw the forgiveness of God.

I remember that at this time I was especially struck with the scene when Christ stood before Pilate. Here was the most absurd contradiction: man judging God, the source of all reality—and judging, not intensely or passionately, but with a casual expedience. In Christ as he stood before Pilate, I could see God accepting us, even while in most of our living we ignore Him.

The point which revealed to me the full depth of Divine love was not, however, Jesus' behavior in his relations with men, but was God's own basic act of joining Himself with our humanity in the Person of Christ. In this act of personal Incarnation, I saw God's attempt to establish with us an intimate relationship of loving communion simply for our beatitude. I realized that through God's grace we now may not only glorify Him, but also enjoy Him forever.

In the light of God's Incarnation, sin took on a new and more terrible dimension, standing not just as the violation of God's proper honor and magnificence, but also as the violation of His loving personal concern for us. Yet the monstrosity of our evil is always exceeded by the mystery of God's mercy. However deep our sin, God's forgiveness always has a deeper measure. However low we fall, Christ's gracious love is always underneath us to support us.

More important, though not as startling, as the experience of forgiveness, in Christ I had a sense of a genuine rebirth. God in Christ not merely accepts us in our evil and sympathizes, but His power begins actively to work within us in order to overcome the evil there, and to free us from the demonic forces that pervade nature and society. Above all, the power of His grace releases us from the dominion of death. The fact of the Resurrection was for me the capstone of the Christian revelation, for here I saw that God affirms us into eternity, that in truth we are carried up by the sheer mystery of His love into the order of life which is properly His.

It was in the genuine humanity of Jesus that God's grace fully realized its restoring power. He was the new man, constituted here on earth, and resurrected to an eternal communion with God. In this new humanity, with its purity from sin and its power of love, we all may participate, in the communion of faith. Jesus Christ is our salvation, being the act of God which overcomes the evil in our midst and builds us anew, and being also the object of this act, the new man, who, raised to the presence of the Father, carries us with him.

The apprehension of this unexpected and totally undeserved grace drew from me, as from most believers, an overwhelming sense of gratitude. With the knowledge that the Lord Almighty affirms and loves us, a deep isolation in the depths of our personalities is dissolved. If God is for us, who can be against us [see Romans 8:31b]? Nothing, not even ourselves. Graced with this confidence, we experience a new freedom to open ourselves to reality, to participate positively and creatively in life. When we see that our sufficiency is from God, and does not hang on our own excellence, we can face the awful depths of our sins without the anxiety that brings self-deception. We are capable of genuine maturity. Resting in the power of God's grace, we are freed from the compulsion to defend our ego against the selfishness of our neighbors. We can expose our sinful selves to them with a new sincerity; we can participate in their lives with a new freedom. Confident of God's love for us and assured that He understands our temptations and agonies from our point of view, we can offer to Him for the first time a genuine prayer—a genuine heartfelt desire really to want to do His will, because it is His.

These were some of the elements in my own response to Christ, and under the impact of this experience I lost all concern for physics. I felt the deepest desire to make my life a direct response to the love of God in Christ, but I had no idea as to how I should realize this desire in the concrete activities of our society. I decided, therefore, after graduation from college to work for a year, and to take time to get used to the fact of Christ and to the entirely new universe he had made of this world.

San Francisco

I went to San Francisco, where I worked as a gas station attendant and taxi driver, and I came to understand better the meaning of the love of neighbor in the light of Christ. I lived in a cheap boarding house, and the great spiritual realities there were boredom and loneliness. The entire life of this group of people was without root and without purpose. They received no mail, knew of no personal attachments, worked in unskilled jobs where they were readily replaceable, and had not a single person who cared one way or the other for their existence.

They struggled against this spiritual misery and isolation in two pathetic ways: with illusions fostered by liquor, and with the communion of sexual intercourse. As I had accepted the popular view that drunkards and prostitutes were unnatural, perverted creatures, twisted by the power of the body over the spirit, it was a startling discovery to find that liquor and sex were the answers to the same spiritual predicament that led others, like myself, to respectability.

In the presence of the appalling loneliness of these people, I realized more clearly how deep in every heart is the yearning to be close to another, to enjoy his presence and to share in the vitality of his experience, and how the everyday life of most men is a misdirected attempt to satisfy this yearning. I came to see that in order to have a genuine brotherly love and sharing of life with others we must do two very difficult things. First, we must open ourselves to the other person, offering our whole being—with its good and evil accretions—for him to behold. It is in this respect that confession is such a vital element in true friendship. But only the strongest confidence in the present working of God's grace in us can bring us to expose to others our own sinful spirits.

Second, the love of neighbor, in addition to self-opening, involves the positive acceptance of the other person, for we can never participate in the more intimate and human regions of his life if we are concerned to judge him. This attitude of acceptance must go all the way, and be independent of the other person's unstable loyalty; we must be able to accept him even when he refuses to forgive us.

Thus a genuine love of neighbor, bringing us, as it does, face to face with the sin in ourselves and others, can grow only in response to God's forgiveness and redemption in Christ. Our sharing of each other must be grounded in a common devotion to a third. Only with the assurance that God forgives us and our neighbor can we forgive. Only under the hope in God's redeeming work, by which we regard no one from a human point of view but as a new creation [see 2 Corinthians 5:16–17], can we wholesomely participate in each other's lives.

During my year in San Francisco, I came to feel that my service lay in ministering the gospel, and to prepare for this I entered the Yale Divinity School.

Yale Divinity School

By this time my initial amazement at the fact of Christ had worn off, and I became increasingly aware of how bitter is redemption for the self-centered soul. When we receive an act of unexpected kindness, we may resent the obligation which this imposes on us. To an infinitely higher degree the free love of Almighty God in Christ chains us with an infinite obligation that infuriates our autonomous spirits. To give up control over our own destiny, to lose the self-satisfaction of gaining our own good, to realize the falsity of our own judgments of right and wrong, to surrender our creativity to God's will, to let the props of self-control and self-respect and self-consistency slip out from under us—this seems like a frightening kind of death and self-denial to the old man in us. The soul, therefore, takes a short cut around the attitude of utter trust in God; it tries by the most subtle self-deception to make use of His forgiveness to bolster its own ego.

In the face of this persistence of sin, I came to realize the cardinal place of repentance in the Christian life. The content of our devotion and the motive of our action are a fusion of gratitude and repentance. We rejoice and sorrow at the same time, in a way the world cannot understand. The will's inner reluctance to yield itself to God makes the Christian way stringent and difficult, so that growth is measured by our willingness to accept at deeper and deeper levels the frustration of our own wills.

The Whitneyville Church

By participating, while at the Divinity School, in the worship and activities of the Whitneyville Congregational Church, I gained my first continuing experience within the life of the church. Here I saw more clearly that Jesus Christ must be the nerve center, the taproot and substance of the church's existence. Only insofar as Christ is the point of response does a church exist at all.

Some of those active in the church may not have Christ as any part of their motivation, so that they are not members of his Body, nor do they participate in his new humanity. Those who in faith do participate, however, even if they do not belong to any church institution, find definite fruits of the Holy Spirit in their lives. An element of repentant humility is introduced into their attitude toward themselves; a frankness and compassionate responsiveness enter their social relations; and above all they live with a slight but saving detachment from the desperation and false gods of our society.

These inner spiritual fruits, of course, cannot be identified with any pattern of external behavior, which is probably why so many in Christ do not consciously realize that they have these gifts. Only the saint—if anyone—can tell which souls are in Christ, for the distinguishing marks are of such a subtly spiritual kind that most of us are insensitive to them.

Because my own development occurred largely apart from a church context, it was not until my experience at Whitneyville that I recognized the essentially corporate character of the Christian life. It is really impossible to worship God except with reference to and in communion with our neighbors. Because God is "our Father," and because Christ died, not for us individually, but for us in our togetherness, each of us feels sorrow, not just for his own sin, but also for the sins of the whole church. He repentantly seeks God's forgiveness for "our trespasses [Matthew 6:12, Luke 11:4]," not simply his own. And he asks the Lord to "deliver *us* from evil [Matthew 6:13]." He prays always with the consciousness of and in communion with all believers, living and dead, because the Lord to whom he prays is the Lord of one Body.

It seems to me that the vibrant life of this one Body lies within the individual congregations, as they respond to Christ in the social tissues of their daily living, and therefore I find in the Congregational Church the most adequate polity. The minister, as a member of the worshipping body, does not mediate or arrange or produce its response. His own life is part of that response, and his service to his parishioners consists in persistently directing their attention to Christ, and in bringing their response to higher self-consciousness in as many areas of their daily life as he can penetrate. Upon that response he must rely for his power to discipline them and to oppose all attempts to subvert any part of the church's life to some false god.

My Personal Vocation

In his response to the Lord a man must try to serve creatively in the particular social situation that he knows, and every pastor stamps his ministry with a radically unique cast. In my own case I see a call to serve the worshipping church in a college community, teaching the subjects of religion and possibly literature from a Christian perspective.

Because college life does not consist simply of reading books, and because the student, like everyone, has a need for worship of which the church must make him conscious, I seek the ordination of my church. At some colleges the religious life is without direction, and in all colleges, it seems to me, Christian devotion is enriched when the teacher of religion is not a man with Christian theories only, but is one who shares with the students the sacraments of the Word and Lord's Supper, and who participates in the life of the association of churches. Many Christian teachers have pastorates in conjunction with their college work, and Mr. Fuller[1] has called my attention to the

[1] The Revd. Charles Floyd Fuller was Minister, Whitneyville Congregational Church, Ham-

real need for teachers of religion to participate in the pastoral work, and join in the full range of the church's life.

But whatever the needs of the particular situation in which I am placed, I hope the Lord will enable me to share our common joy in Christ, through the ministry and fellowship of our churches.

---

den, Connecticut, from 1943 to 1958. McGill was ordained here, 11 May, 1952. The church was formed in 1794 and became Whitneyville United Church of Christ in 1957.

Appendix 2

Faculty of Divinity—Memorial Minute

Arthur C. McGill: 7 August 1926–10 September 1980

At a meeting of the Faculty of Divinity on April 18,
1983, the following Minute was placed upon the records

Arthur C. McGill's memorial minute would be, had its authors the capacity, a verbal portrait of Arthur rather than a brief, conventional biography offering a chronological record of his intellectual and professional development and accomplishments; such a portrait would best correspond to Arthur's own convictions, and to his style of teaching and writing, for Arthur deeply believed that each human life is a mystery that cannot be properly presented simply as a careful arrangement of objective facts. Arthur himself possessed the exceptional gift of treating subject matter ostensibly familiar in such fresh and original ways that to listen to him attentively was akin to finding oneself being reoriented in a reality one had hitherto taken for granted.

All who knew Arthur well, particularly in his final years, remember especially the courage and creativity with which he faced the death that he knew was soon to come. He had been plagued for most of his life with diabetes, and during the last few years his physical condition deteriorated visibly and rapidly, to the point that he required a kidney transplant in 1978, an operation in 1978, an operation from which he never fully recovered. Those of us who watched Arthur's illness—an illness that was in fact his dying—at close hand could not help but admire the indomitable spirit with which he met each new day, and each new setback.

■ ■ ■

He never complained about what was happening to him. Instead, he focused his attention and interest on what was going on about him, on the friends that were with him for that moment, and he was always ready with questions about what had recently happened to his visitors or to their loved ones.

Arthur was a man who genuinely cared for others, and he expressed that interest and concern on every occasion of meeting.

As his body increasingly failed him and he was often in and out of the hospitals, Arthur's thoughts and words—and his Divinity School courses—turned frequently to the questions of suffering and death, while he prepared himself, in his inner aloneness, for what he was certain would not be long in coming. Characteristically, this reflection was no morbid inward-turning of self-pity; on the contrary, he used the experience of his last sickness as an opportunity for fresh thinking, to develop a theology of poverty, suffering, and dying which he could pass on to his students. At this time he set down some of his most trenchant thoughts on the meaning of life in the form of meditations on what it means to be a person who is a patient destined to encounter the reality that the medical profession cannot acknowledge—the reality of death. His reflection on the life and death of Jesus, particularly as set out in the Gospel according to John, let him to see death as a kind of "transitive giving" of new life and nourishment to the living.

Arthur's own actions, as well as his ideas, expressed this conviction. His students reported the overwhelming impression made on them when he found it necessary to lecture one day from a lawn chair. The topic of the lecture: the Christian understanding of suffering. We should not misread this concentration on suffering and death as if it were a rationalizing and justifying of his personal fate. Arthur's personal experience never became the center or topic of his theological inquiry; it served rather as the occasion for his thinking. Nor did his concern with these matters cause him to lose perspective on other great themes of theology; his last manuscript was on the theme of *glory*.

Arthur McGill was a stimulating and provocative theological controversialist. His comments on a historical figure, like Athanasius or Anselm (both favorites of his), always opened dimensions of meaning that others had somehow overlooked. He could also work the same magic on contemporary theology, such as that of Karl Barth, on which he wrote a brilliant doctoral thesis. And his creative interpretations of traditional Christian doctrines—the doctrine of the trinity or original sin—consistently brought out in quite unexpected ways new insights into human existence or into the meaning of faith in God—not just in general, but in relation to the particular problems of contemporary individual and social life.

Arthur was a master of the pointed phrase that conveyed in a striking manner, one felt, precisely what he wished to say and that gave his hearers the sense of being allowed a glimpse of deeply hidden mysteries of truth. But he was neither a ponderous nor a somber man. Especially in his earlier years, he was a great storyteller and practical joker. He had a unique sense of humor, and he was always able to laugh at himself—even in tragic circumstances. With what great hilarity he told the story, a year or so before his death, of the several hours spent in the Somerville jail when the police mistook his condition of insulin shock for public drunkenness.

Arthur Chute McGill was born in Wolfville, Nova Scotia on August 7, 1926, to Chester and Marjorie McGill. He grew up in the Boston area and received an A.B. in physics from Harvard University in 1948. After a summer driving a taxicab in San Francisco, he entered Yale Divinity School, from which he received the B.D. degree in 1951. Later that year he married Lucille Orner, and in due course they had three children.

Arthur was ordained into the Congregational ministry, but he continued his graduate study in theology, and in 1961 he received his Ph.D. from Yale University. From 1952 to 1957 Arthur taught, first at Amherst College, then at Wesleyan University. He was a Fulbright Scholar at the University of Louvain, Belgium in 1958, returning to the U.S. to teach at Princeton University where he remained for nine years. He then spent a sabbatical year in London and delivered the Cadbury Lectures at the University of Birmingham in 1969, returning to the United States to teach at Harvard Divinity School as Bussey Professor of Theology until his death, September 10, 1980.

Arthur's main professional life was given over to university teaching, for which he was awarded a number of prizes. He was also in demand as a guest minister at churches around the country, and he was a founding member of the Ecumenical Institute for Advanced Theological Research in Jerusalem. His publications include: *Reason in a Violent World*, *The Celebration of Flesh*, *The Many-Faced Argument* (with John Hick), and *Suffering: A Test of Theological Method*.

■ ■ ■

Both Arthur's teaching and his writing manifested a powerful drive toward bringing some kind of connectedness and order into what he felt was a fragmented and disintegrating world. He sought to keep his theological reflection in close connection both with his modern science—in which he took his undergraduate degree, and which remained a lifelong interest—and modern poetry, which he often recited in a striking way in lectures, and to which he devoted an interpretive book, *The Celebration of Flesh*; but above all he was concerned that his theological reflection not become abstract and filled with generalities but be a vivid and significant illumination of concrete human existence, of the sufferings and joys, the hopes and fears, the frustrations and achievements of everyday life.

All this he understood in terms of a pervasive dialectic of weakness and power, human frailty and divine glory, which was rooted in Paul's interpretation of the Gospel. Religion, as he understood it, was "the human response to the superb powers from which man sees himself and his communities deriving life and death," but academic inquiry all too often excludes these phenomena and questions as unimportant or irrelevant, concentrating instead "on certain sets of objects defined in terms of their own natures." All such movements he criticized and rejected as contributing to the victimization of humans in the modern world.

■ ■ ■

In articulating these views he drew upon existentialist, humanist, liberal and Marxist critiques, but he refused to share in the ideological self-righteousness of any of these movements, which so often seem to value their own conceptual formulations—with their potentialities for predication and control of human affairs—more highly than the concrete needs of actual victimized persons. All systematic philosophies and ideologies, whether religious or secular, were much too programmatic for his taste. Arthur understood the biblical concept of sin as referring to "the condition of terrible victimization" by "inhuman powers from which [people] cannot escape," and these powers, in his view, were just as often exercised through such media as systematic thinking or bureaucratic organization as they were through disease, war, and accident.

Although Arthur was an intensely private person who either by design or disposition carefully concealed his inmost self from even his closet friends, he could also give himself freely and unselfishly for the nourishment and healing of those immediately confronting him, a stance which especially endeared him to his close circle of students. An example from the last period of his life well reveals his openness and undefensiveness. His students wanted to record his lectures, and asked him to edit the transcriptions so they would be completely accurate. He was willing to have them make a transcription of his lectures, but he insisted the students themselves should do any editing they thought appropriate. The important thing to preserve was what they had found significant, not what he supposed himself to have given them.

Arthur McGill was a man much loved by those who knew him well; and he will be long remembered. "The Lord gave, and the Lord hath taken away; blessed be the name of the Lord."

Dieter Georgi
Gordon D. Kaufman
Richard R. Niebuhr

With appreciation to Gordon D. Kaufman and the Harvard Gazette *for permission to publish this "Memorial Minute."*